The Gospel
in NUMBERS

The Gospel in NUMBERS

By

Henry Law

This book was written in the prevailing style of that period. Language and spelling have been left original in an effort to give the full flavor of this classic work.

Bottom of the Hill Publishing

Memphis, TN

www.BottomoftheHillPublishing.com

ISBN: 978-1-61203-788-2

Content

THE NUMBERED PEOPLE

"Take a census of the whole Israelite community by their clans and families, listing every man by name, one by one. You and Aaron are to number by their divisions all the men in Israel twenty years old or more who are able to serve in the army." Numbers 1:2-3

These verses bring us to the camp of Israel still circling Sinai's base. Christian thought--waiting for dews of heavenly grace--delights to linger here. Let us observe the people closely. They are snatched by God's hand from tyrannizing foes. A miracle of care supplies their daily needs. A moving pillar guides their way. The law has been repeated to them amid terrific phenomena. Moreover they are fenced around by strict peculiarities of social custom and of typical worship. Their contact with the world is broken. They move amid the nations of the earth, as a stream flowing through the ocean's bed, unmingling with contiguous waves. God near, with sheltering arms, is their defense. Goodness and mercy guard their present steps. The land of promised rest is the horizon of their hopes.

Reader, these annals are a historic mirror. They picture a heavenly Father's special dealings with each child of faith. In every age and place there is an Israel thus mercifully loved, and led, and fed. The antitype will never fail, until the last Christian's course is run.

Hence precious teaching meets us in the study of this chart. We often err and fail, through dim discernment of our state. Peace would abound, and comforts cheer, and strength put forth more vigor, if right perceptions shed a clearer light. Let us, then, *view ourselves* in Israel's varied story. Our every step finds counterpart in them.

The parallel is quickly drawn. They once groaned bitterly in cruel bondage. But mercy set them free. Believer, you too were once a slave at Satan's will. He ruled you with an iron yoke. But now the chain is broken, and you rejoice, the ransomed freed-man of the Lord. Egypt is escaped. The tyrants holds you not.

Israel's tribes are journeying, as strangers, through a desert-waste. And is not yours a wilderness-wandering? The abiding country is not here. The rest is far away. But they are escorted and protected by a heavenly guide. So, too, a beckoning hand marks out your wanderings by day--by night. Is your soul needy? The bread of life fails not. Are you athirst? The wells of life are ever open.

They had heard "the voice of words"--the fiery law. This law has also pierced the deep recesses of your inner man. You have thus learned the glorious righteousness of God--the hateful sinfulness of sin--your ruined state in SELF. You hence are taught to prize the grace of your curse-bearing Lord, and the rich worth of His imputed merits.

Was Israel God's special portion? You, too, are not your own. You are a purchased property--a peculiar race. You shun the world, as a forbidden path--a rebel camp--an uncongenial climate--an alien tribe--a Jael's tent--a land of filth and snares.

This is a scanty outline. Daily experience fills in the picture. Let each similitude be traced. For each is a fruitful school of wisdom and improvement. There is, indeed, no novel thought in this recital. Each Bible-reader knows these things. But common truths--like common blessings--soon lose their point. Colors soon fade, without renewing touch. The flame expires, without reviving breath. Reader, be wise, and often trace your own case in this predictive story.

And now, before the people move, God speaks again. He gives command to register the Number of each tribe. Account must be distinctly taken. All names must be recorded. Their multitudes must all be reckoned and exactly known.

New instruction meets us here. God ever leads us in a brightening path. Fresh dealings are fresh seeds of wisdom. They call us to discern anew His mind. May, then, this Numbering-act enrich faith's stores!

In common matters, men count possessions, which are *choice, and dear, and prized.* They, whose base joys are fixed on this world's pelf--thus calculate their gold. Their coffers are often opened. Frequent reckonings review the contents. See, too, the watchful shepherd's care. His marking eye perpetually surveys the flock. As they go forth--as they return--the Number is most diligently kept.

Do we, then, stray beyond sound limits--do we indulge unfounded fancy--when in God's Numbering we read God's love? Do not clear characters here write, that His people are thus Numbered, because loved--counted, because prized? This truth extends to all the children of faith's family. My soul, come bow before it. Its worth exceeds all worlds.

There is no blessedness like his, whose glowing gratitude often realizes, My God loves me--my name is in His heart. The Lord of all creation esteems me among His choicest jewels.

The knowledge of this fact is reached by happy steps. They are all scripturally firm. Review them. **Why** was Jesus sent to bear your sins, and deck you in His robe of righteousness? Why did Jehovah inflict on Him the hell-pains, which were justly yours? Why was Christ slain? Why are you spared? There can be only one reply, 'God loves you'.

And why did the Spirit speed to arouse your sleeping conscience--to show self's ruin, and the remedy of the Cross? Why did your inward adamant dissolve, and unbelief melt into faith, and your whole heart clasp Jesus, as its own? There can be only one reply, 'God loves you'.

How is it, that your slender bark still rides above the raging billows of an engulfing world? How is it, that your tottering feet are still upheld along the slippery hill, which leads to Zion's heights? The *strength* is not your own. It is most freely given. There can be only one reply, 'God loves you'.

When did this love commence?--Tell me, when God began to be, and I will tell you, when His love began. Will not this love expire? Can God be no more God? While God is God, He must be love.

God loves you! Would that the eye of faith forever rested on this glorious truth! Heroic might will brace the inner man, just as this thrives and strengthens. God loves you! What an amazing impulse to bear the willing servant over all mountains of doubt, and fear, and hindrance! God loves you! What a strong shield to ward off Satan's darts! God loves you! It is victory, before one blow is struck. It is a pillow of unfailing peace. It is light in the dark day of trial. It is a cordial of invigorating comfort. It is the holy wing to lift above the world. It is an foretaste of a sure heaven.

Next, **who** are Numbered? The young--the weak--the female--stand apart. None are enrolled, but those whose age and strength enable them for WAR.

Christ's service is a mighty work--a valiant struggle--a determined fight. *Satan* disputes each onward step. We must undauntedly resist. The *world* presents its countless troops--all quick to wound--and skilled to capture. We must defy them with unwavering front. The *flesh* is an internal foe--haunting the secret chambers of the heart, and entwined around our very being. It gives no respite. No respite must be given to it.

Believer, yours is this warrior-life. Fight, as one fighting for eternity. Strive, as one striving for a kingdom. March, as one resolute to take heaven by storm. Jesus calls--commands--precedes. Follow Him boldly. The Numbered host is Numbered for the fight. The fighting host will soon shout, Victory. No one will triumph, who has never fought. No one, who truly fights, will fail. Each Numbered soldier paid a **ransom price**. Ex. 30:12. The rich--the poor--were equally assessed. There was no difference for differing age or state.

The Gospel of this fact is clear. All in Christ's camp are ransomed by His blood. All join the chosen band, confessing, that they need redemption, and glorying in redemption found. All plead one sacrifice. All bring the same expiation-price.

Next count the register. It presents a vast array of Numbered warriors. They stretch beyond six hundred thousand men. Numb. 1:46. Whence is this marvelous increase? One family had entered Egypt. Hardship, and cruelty, and toil had done their worst to keep them low. But now, within the lapse of a short period, they stand an army of this vast extent. Whence is this multiplied expanse?

God's early promise was their portion. "I will make of you a great nation." Gen. 12:2. God's purpose never fails. When He has spoken, seeming impossibilities may rise--but all in vain--fulfillment will not tarry. The Numbered People prove, that our God is Truth as well as Love. His promise is a seed, which surely ripens into fruit.

Reader, behold again this multitude. It is an emblem of a far larger host. The conflict will soon end; and then before the throne a countless company will be spread. Rev. 7:9. They are the saved from every nation--kindred--people--tongue. Their robes are white; for Jesus's blood has washed them. Their hands wave palms; for they have conquered in His name. Say--say--will you rejoice and triumph with them? Say--say--are you now warring, a comrade in these ranks? The *fight* is prelude to the *crown*.

About a year has passed since the last Numbering of this family. The Levites then formed part of the collected mass. They are not now included. They stand apart, a separate portion. But mark a wondrous fact. The Number then and now amounts exactly to the same. Israel has surrendered Levi's tribe, but Israel's forces are not thereby less. Here is a profitable lesson. We never lose by giving to the Lord. Selfishness is poverty. Christian benevolence is wealth. We often grudgingly withhold. The result is loss, not gain. The coffers drain not, which supply God's cause. The more thus given is the more possessed. They, who thus lay out, lay up.

Reader, once more survey the Numbered People. You are inclined to say, this band will safely reach the promised land. Surely their willing steps will ever run in the appointed way. Alas! two, and two only, steadfastly adhere. The multitude distrust the Lord. They willfully provoke Him. Therefore just indignation dooms them to exclusion. Their corpses strew the desert. And one by one they line the road with graves. They fall, a dreadful proof, that **outward privileges alone** do not save. Unbelief nullified their many means of grace. It poisoned their cup of blessing. "They could not enter in, because of unbelief." Heb. 3:19.

Ah, unbelief! It is the sin of sins--the misery of miseries--the hopeless malady--the death of souls--the bar, which shuts out Christ.

Reader, is this vile viper lurking in your heart? Oh! drag it to the cross, and slay it there. Implore the Spirit, by His mighty sword, to hew it into shreds. If it survives, you die. The case is clear. Can he be healed, who scorns the only cure? Can he reach home, who leaves the only homeward path? Can he be cleansed, who flees the only cleansing stream? Can he go in, who will not pass the door? Can he escape from the fast-sinking wreck, who spurns the life-boat? Who can reach God, who puts aside the Mediator? Who can be saved, who tramples down the only Savior? Unbelief rejects the Gospel, and so perishes. It turns God's truth into a lie, and it goes hence to learn its folly, where faith never comes. Many may be Numbered, as the Church's sons, who are not Numbered, as the heirs of life.

THE CAMP

*"Each tribe will be assigned its own area in **the camp**, and the various groups will camp beneath their family banners. The Tabernacle will be located at the center of these tribal compounds."* Numbers 2:2

When Balaam looks down upon the outstretched Camp of Israel, his very soul expands. It must break forth in praise. The beauty captivates. The order charms. The evidence is clear--no common people there reside. He rapturously exclaims, "How beautiful are your tents, O Jacob, your dwelling places, O Israel!" He paints a landscape of delights. "They spread before me like groves of palms, like fruitful gardens by the riverside. They are like aloes planted by the Lord, like cedars beside the waters." Numb. 24:5, 6. Images of choice fruits--elaborate arrangement--luxuriance--verdure--stateliness--fragrance--lend colors to depict the scene.

Reader, let us, too, mount the heights of godly meditation, and in spirit view this favored Camp. And as we gaze, may rays from heaven illumine every part!

The points rich in instruction are--the tents themselves--their order--position--standard.

1. THE TENTS. Abodes present themselves. They are not splendid palaces, and golden columns, and sparkling capitals, and giant pyramids. They are not constructed, as lasting monuments to future times.

The simple contrast meets the eye. They are poor tents. They stand today. Tomorrow sees the cords relaxed--the fastenings removed, and a vacant place. They are the pilgrim-dwellings of a pilgrim-troop--the short-lived homes of short-lived sojourners.

This first view instantly reminds of mortal state. What is our body? It is nothing but clay. These frames have one origin--the dust. The vilest reptile and the proudest prince are composites of one poor mire. Is it not folly, then, to pamper and admire this flesh? At best these bodies are a tent--than which creation knows no humbler thing.

How soon they crumble! No care--no thought--no art can lengthen out continuance. The countless families of foregone ages--where are they now? Dust they were. To dust they are gone back.

The many families of this our day--where do they speed? Dust they are--to dust they hasten. The tents must fall. But when? Perchance this very hour. Is he not then the fool of fools, who boasts him of to-morrow's dawn!

My soul, from Israel's tents, you learn, *how fleeting is life's day!* Press then the question, 'When I go hence, is an abiding mansion mine? There is a kingdom prepared from the foundation of the world. Is it for me? Christ lives to prepare everlasting homes. Are they for me? Oh! turn not from this Camp, until faith clearly reads its title to the heavenly home.

Flesh is a *lowly* abode. This thought commends the grace of Jesus. He scorned not to assume it. Amazing fact! He took this clothing, as His own. Beneath these *rags* He hid the glories of His glorious Deity. No man was ever man more thoroughly than Jesus. He tabernacled in manhood's baseness, as truly as He shone in Godhead's brightness. He thus descended, that He might endure--suffer--bleed--die--might bear the curse--and hang upon the cross.

This none but man could do, therefore His tent was pitched, as man, among the sons of men. He was made *man,* that He might be made *sin.* He was made sin, that He might take it thoroughly away. He sought a lowly tent (body) to do a godlike work.

But soon the degradation passed. Humiliation's valley was left. The cross was triumph's chariot. And now in heaven--at God's right hand--on glory's throne--the God-man sits. Manhood now shines in Him arrayed in light of Deity. And all, whom faith makes one with Him, will soon behold and share this luster. Their vile bodies shall be changed. Weakness and frailty shall put on unfading freshness. The lowly bud shall bloom into a glorious flower. The glorious Head will leave no member in decay.

Blessed are they, whose faith discerns Him nailed as their Surety on the tree. He comes--He quickly comes to gild mortality with life. Happy the inhabitants of these crumbling frames, if only they are Christ's! They now are vilest dust. They soon will shine more brightly than ten thousand suns.

2. THE ORDER. Let Israel's Camp be now more closely scanned. What perfect regularity appears! Rule draws each line. Arrangement is complete. These streets of tents are uniformity's perfection.

One truth is here distinctly written. Our God delights in order. Where He presides, confusion vanishes.

Is it not so in every Christian heart? When Jesus takes the throne, wise rule prevails. Disturbing lusts lie down. Perplexing doubts flee far. Gusts of sinful desire are lulled. The soul is like the well-set garden, in which *method* plants each shrub and flower.

Is it not so in Christian life? Each duty occupies its stated post. There is no tangled labyrinth of plans--no misspent diligence--no toil without a purpose. God's worship has its sacred place--and no intruder interferes. The Scripture claims appointed study--and then the door is barred against disturbing entrance. The family demands due care--due care is given. The home--the closet--the public--the world, in turn have claims--in turn are served. Each morning dawns--each evening closes, on a well-ordered scheme of work.

How different is the worldling's day! It seems an upset hive. The notes all jar--movements all jostle. It is a jumbled chaos of desire--attempt--design. Motives conflict with motives--thoughts with thoughts--plans with plans. Why is it so? God rules not. Wisdom holds not the rudder. Therefore the ship is sport to every wind and wave. There is no order, but in the Camp of God.

But in Israel's Camp each tribe has its place. The family of Aaron guard the tabernacle's door. The sons of Levi encircle the holy tent. The other tribes occupy appointed ground. God fixes all the bounds, and all the bounds are gladly kept.

The same all-ruling mind disposes now each member of Christ's body. Each enters on the stage of life, as God is pleased to call. Each runs a pre-ordained course. Each disappears, when the allotted task is done. We see this clear arrangement throughout the Church's history. At the set time the sun of *Moses* sets--the star of *Joshua* dawns--the several *Judges* rule--the several *kings* ascend the throne. In the right season Paul labors--and *apostles* preach--and *martyrs* seal the truth with blood--and each devoted *teacher* toils--and each disciple aids the Gospel-cause. God plans each champion's station in the Gospel-Camp.

Reader, bow humbly before this ordering mind. Then discontent will not arise. No murmurings will mourn an obscure lot--a grievous burden--a lengthened pilgrimage--or an early grave. The time--the task--the place--will be regarded, as most wisely fixed. What if self-will could make a change? Would it not mar the work on earth, and tarnish the eternal crown? The foot should not desire the hand's employ--or the eye's higher seat. Ephraim is pleased, that Judah leads. Judah would not take Ephraim's rear place.

3. THE POSITION. But all these tents share one grand privilege. "Around the *Tent of Meeting* shall they camp." They all have common focus. As the planets circle the sun, so these surround the sanctuary. *God is the center.* They form the wide circumference. And from each door one sight--the holy tent--is visible.

Is there no *meaning* here? There is!--and it is *precious.* God in Christ Jesus is the center--the heart--the life--the strength--the shield--the joy of His believing flock. In their midst He dwells--their glory and delight. When they go forth, their eyes are fixed on Him. When they return, it is to nestle round His presence.

Is there no *warning* here? There is!--and it is *wise.* Let Christians ponder this Camp's plan, when called to fix their dwellings upon earth. When weighing the advantages of the right place to settle, the foremost thought should be, 'Is God known here? Are His pure truths here clearly taught?' There may be rites and forms. But an external rituals are not grace. A heaven-directed church spire leads not infallibly to heaven. 'Ichabod' is the name, if God in Christ be not proclaimed.

Soul-profit is real profit. And soul-profit cannot be apart from Christ. Soul-loss is saddest loss--and the soul loses, when not led to Christ. Our children, too, and all who form our household, claim, that their first good be first considered. Was Lot a gainer, when his eye only coveted the fertile plains? How David's pious spirit mourns, when exiled from the house of God! Can fairer fields, or sweeter temporal prospects, make amends for a cold blank within? Can healthful air repay for inward sickness and a spiritual decline? What, if any tribe should have receded to spots, from which the cloud could not be seen! The end would have been sure. It was cut off from Israel. So all, who willingly abide far from the Gospel's light, choose present darkness leading to far darker night.

4. THE BANNER. A banner floats above each tribe. Beneath the well-known sign they rest. And by its side they march.

Believers have a banner too. The banner over them is Jesus's love. Song 2:4. Enlightened eyes can ever catch these waving flag folds, and read therein the great Commander's heart.

The banner is a pledge of **safety**. True, mighty foes hate and assail. True, night and day they plot and rage, and draw the bow, and lay the snare. But they must fail. The fight may be both fierce and long, but in Christ's Camp no follower can finally expire.

Beneath it there is **sweet repose**. The weary spirit and the worn-out flesh can often watch no more. Unless the vigilance of heavenly love defend, surprise will overpower the fainting bands. But as is the vineyard of the Lord, so is His Camp. "I, the Lord, will watch over it and tend its fruitful vines. Each day I will water them; day and night I will watch to keep enemies away." Isaiah 27:3

Beside it there is **victory**. Many have fought beneath the Gospel-banner, and all have triumphed. They, who go boldly forward, looking unto Jesus, assuredly prevail. Paul lifts aloud the happy cry--"Thanks be to God, who always makes us to triumph in Christ." 2 Cor. 2:14. What is the one testimony of the saints in light? We strove and conquered "by the blood of the Lamb." We waved His banner and now we wave these palms. We clung to it, and now we wear these crowns. Happy Camp, where Jesus is Salvation's Captain--His cross salvation's banner--His heaven salvation's rest!

Believer, glory in your banner, and be steadfast. Alas! Sometimes shame, and timidities, and fears, have caused ignoble tremblings, and flights, and falls. Peter denied his noble flag. Deep was his wound, and bitter his repenting sighs. His warning cries, "Be courageous. Be strong." Demas was allured, and left the ranks. Was he recovered from the world's embrace? The all-revealing day alone can tell. But that dread time will show a cowardly troop bewailing the hour, when they deserted Christ. Cling, then, cling boldly, constantly, to Him. Let every company--moment--place--witness your firm resolves. Wave now and ever the glorious banner--"Christ is all."

Thus dwell within the Camp, and you will reign upon the throne.

THE NAZARITE

*"This is the law of **the Nazarite**."* Numb. 6:21

Here a new ordinance appears. It seems a special flower set by God's hand within the garden of the Jewish code. Therefore let special fragrance now be sought by faith, for surely special fragrance may be found.

Israel's whole race was severed from the world. But the wide circumference encompassed a narrower circle. Where all were separate, the Nazarites occupied special separation.

These stood apart, as a peculiar dedication to the Lord. Amid surrounding columns they rose the highest pyramids. Among God's servants they wore distinctive clothing. Where all were nationally holy, they showed the holiest badge.

They bound themselves by voluntary vows. Some mighty motive must have urged their hearts. But it is not revealed. Conjecture may suppose, but cannot be assured. The vow might be the act of men weighed down by consciousness of sin--appalled by sight of inborn evil--or penitent for grievous falls. It might be gratitude for signal mercies. It might be zeal to arouse others to think more of God. But the real cause is veiled. This only is declared, that Nazarites, obeying a strong impulse, gave themselves peculiarly to God.

My soul, the Nazarite here speaks with warning voice to you. Your days, are they devoted service? Your public walk, is it resplendent godliness? Are all observers led to mark, that you are wholly God's? But surely above all you should be pre-eminently His.

Think of His dealings with you--His tender love--and smiles of never-failing care. Think of your Jesus--His cross--His blood--His wounds--His agonies. Think of the mercy-seat--the interceding prayer--the coming glory--the eternity of bliss. Think of hell merited, and heaven your free-grace home. Surely each morn should see you self-bound by stricter vow--and dedicated to more signal piety.

The Nazarite's motives are unknown. But Nazarite-rules are rigidly prescribed. They are threefold. Let them now be viewed.

1. No juice of **GRAPE**, no produce of the vine, from seed unto skin, may touch the consecrated lips. Not only the intoxicating

cup is banished far, but all, which grows on the intoxicating tree. Enticement's total troop, from first to last, must be expelled. Like Achan, and his little ones--all must die. Numb. 6:3, 4.

Believer, this principle is broad and deep. You openly avow, that you are not your own. Your body--spirit--mind and soul--are purchased by redeeming blood. They all are bound a living sacrifice to the one altar--Christ. Hence you must keep them pure--clean--bright--strong--vigorous for His work. They should stand, as servants with loins girt--ready at all times to discharge His will.

Then sedulously flee whatever, like the juice of grape, may tend to weaken the firm energy, or to stir up the sleeping brood of sensual and ungodly lusts. Alas! what evil lingers still in every saintly heart! A sudden spark may cause a fearful blaze. Keep far from the beguiling cup.

Touch not the seed or the skin. Flee not strong potions only, but all that may insidiously corrupt the taste. More than gross vice is branded here. Evils may enter in a pigmy form. At first they may seem harmless, as the gentle dove. Avoid them. They are the cancer's touch. They are the weed's first seed. Rapidly they grow. Fatally they spread. Mightily they strengthen. Soon they pervade the weakened soul.

2. No **RAZOR** approaches the Nazarite's hair. His flowing locks openly announce his separate state. His head pre-eminently bears the signal of his service. The dedication must not be a secret act, known only to the conscience and the Lord. The front must witness, that the man is God's. Numb. 6:5.

Believer, here is another lesson for your life. Religion is not for the closet or the knees alone. It is not a lily, growing only in the shade. It is to be the one attire, in which you move abroad--the holy crown of hair, which sparkles on your brow. It must be conspicuous, as locks pendant from the head. It is not to be cut short or hidden. It must arrest attention. Like the flag, it must proclaim the country, to which the ship belongs.

Christian meekness, and the Spirit's wisdom, never conceal our faith. Truth scorns all cowardly modesty. Bold honesty rejects such timid shame. Pure religion shines as the sun without one cloud. Thus others profit by its rays. Thus, like an attractive magnet, it draw souls to God.

3. He must **AVOID ALL CONTACT WITH THE DEAD**. He must not close the eyes of his expiring friends, or catch their parting breath, or bear their corpses to the grave. Among the living, he must live. Where life is absent, he must be absent too. Numb. 6:6,

7.

Why is death to be thus shunned? Reasons are obvious. It is the penalty of sin--the sign of God's most righteous wrath. It is a proof of innocence destroyed--of evil touched--of vengeance merited. It is abomination's colleague. Therefore it is emblem of what holy men should abhor. Life, too, is God's inseparable essence. He cannot die. Therefore to intermix with death, denotes a separation from our God.

Here is again a rule for Christian walk. He, who is Christ's, must flee the touch of everything allied to sin. The holy garments may not be defiled. The blood-washed feet must shun polluted paths. The vessels for the Master's use may have no stain. The spirit's temple must be pure. Corruption in no form may soil it.

Believer, rigidly apply this maxim. It drives you from the contagion of ungodly scenes. How many crowds are nothing but a crowded charnel-house! The bodies breathe, but hold no breathing soul. The words--the works--are odious, as an open grave. Arise--depart. The living dwell not amid tombs. The atmosphere pollutes. Depart, touch not the dead.

How many books are deathful! They may have fascinating garb. But they are only gay, as corpses decked with flowers. Their taint destroys. Their chilly touch corrupts.

This rule brands many a pulpit, as a plague-spot. A lifeless teacher often guides in paths of death. No spark from heaven has vivified his soul. What, then, but putrefaction issues from his lips? *On earth there is not a more pitiable sight, than death, in a preacher's form, digging the grave of souls.*

Here, too, we see the misery of those, who by dead works expect to buy soul-life. All works are dead, which grow not on the stem of faith. Such are but rotten berries. They live not unto God. How can they purchase life?

But no precautionary care can always keep men from the dying scene. Death has an unrestricted range. It moves among the busy haunts. Its icy hand is everywhere. In every spot it seizes victims. Thus the most watchful Nazarite might most unwillingly stand by the dead.

If so, corruption has been by his side--pollution has polluted him--his vow is broken. Therefore atonement must be made. The ordinance now commands him, as guilty, to seek God. He is required to place a whole burnt-offering on the blazing altar. He must then add a sacrifice for sin. Moreover, as a debtor, he must buy remission by a trespass-offering. Thus the chief types, which shadowed out Christ's blood, must all be brought.

This is not all. The former period of his Nazarate is cancelled. The previous days are counted, as lost time. He must cut short the locks, which hitherto had proved his separate state. He must commence afresh his dedicated walk. Numb. 6:9-12.

Hark! What a voice here cries, Beware of sudden evil! Satan is a lurking foe. He shoots his darts from hidden ambushes. When all seems safe, a wound is given. There is a pitfall in the firmest paths. Where least suspected, nets are spread. David arose, unconscious of the slippery ground. A few brief moments rolled him in the mire. But there is hope for suddenly contracted guilt. This type attests this blessed truth. It bids the failing Nazarite to recover his lost state by offerings of blood. Reader, at all times there is an open access to a remitting God. There is a Savior waiting to obliterate. Come, plead His merits--present His expiating death. There is no stain, which He removes not.

The type, moreover, shows, that pardon found must be the starting post of new devotedness. The washed feet ascend anew the holy hill. The cleansed hands fight with more vigor. The Nazarite, passing the appointed gate, enters again upon his sacred course.

These reconciling rites were ordered, if the offence were sudden, unintended, and abhorred. But what, if deliberate transgression be indulged? The ordinance is silent here; and thus warns solemnly. Where shall he turn, who turns presumptuously from God? Where is his hope, who boldly touches sin? Reader, never burst conscience-bounds. Grieve not the Spirit's gentle mind. Drive not the holy inhabitant from your breast. Some, who ran well, have wantonly cast off the gracious yoke. The after-course has been fall upon fall, without a check or turn.

The Nazarite vow continued only for a fixed time. The days expired. The vow was then discharged. The badge of consecration was laid down.

But grand solemnities attested the completion of this hallowed state. The Nazarite enters the tabernacle's gate. He stands beside the sacrificing altar. He brings each victim, which symbolizes sin's desert. No rite is absent, which confesses need of remission, and trust in reconciling blood. A lamb, as a burnt-offering, dies. A lamb again, as a sin-offering, is utterly consumed. A perfect ram, as a peace-offering, solicits peace. Meat-offerings in every form are piled. Drink-offerings in abundance flow. Voluntary gifts profusely follow. All hair is next shorn off. The fire receives it. It ascends in the ascending flame of the peace-offering. Numb. 6:13-21.

But why is there this expenditure of blood? What is the significance of this multitude of rites? They all seek expiation. They all look onward to the cross--and thus they graphically show, that *holiest deeds of holiest men can only find acceptance through the dying Jesus.* For surely this full train of pardon-petitioning sacrifice distinctly states, that the Nazarite's devoted course still needed to be cleansed.

Believer, is not this the conscious feeling of your humbled soul? You are the Lord's. You strive to serve Him--wholly--unreservedly--forever. You would bring to Him your every moment--faculty--and power. You would present the offering of your thoughts--your words--your works. But ah! what failures! You would do good--evil is present. In public acts, what inconsistency! In private duties, what outbreakings of corruption! In the closet, evil thoughts assail. On the knees, the tempter haunts. Some base imagination stains ascending praise. Your self-denial is too often self-indulgence. *The badge of the 'Nazarite vow' too often hides a worldling's heart.* What, then, shall be done? Behold the cross. There is your only help. Thence only is your peace. In that most precious blood you only can obliterate your guilt. Come, wash therein your every duty--service--prayer--thanksgiving. Cleanse there the stains of your most holy hours. Live under vows, as a strict Nazarite. But wrestle for forgiveness, as a sad short-comer.

THE THREEFOLD BLESSING

"The Lord bless you and keep you--the Lord make His face shine upon you, and be gracious unto you; the Lord lift up His countenance upon you, and give you peace." Numb. 6:24-26.

How gracious is our God in Christ! His mercy overtops the heaven of heavens. Throughout the Bible-page, at every turn, it beams forth in fresh rays. Behold a signal instance. He speaks in these verses, and blessings drop from Him, sparkling as the morning dew--large as Jehovah's heart.

The tribes are now prepared to move. The guiding pillar will soon conduct them into desert-paths. Doubtless they go encircled with all pledges of support. Their cup of favor mantles to the brim. But God still multiplies new stores of comfort. He adds--He superadds--vast bounties. He tells, that all, which heaven contains, shall fall in showers upon their heads.

With this loving mind He thus instructs the priests. "This is how you are to bless the Israelites." The act is ordered. "You shall bless." The distinct form of blessing is supplied. "This is how you are to bless." He wills to give. Is not this grace? He wills, that the vast amplitude of His gifts be evidently seen. Is not this grace on grace?

Mark the broad channel of their course. "The Lord bless you, and keep you; the Lord make His face shine upon you, and be gracious unto you; the Lord lift up His countenance upon you, and give you peace." The bounteous God thus opens wide the treasures of His bounty-house--and tells the people, 'All these riches are for you.'

Believer, come now and listen to these sounds, as you sit calmly on your Gospel-heights. You see it is the office of the priest to bless. This introduces Jesus to the eye of faith. He is 'the Church's blessing Priest'. The only priesthood is wrapped up in Him. The earthly office, ministered by men, long since expired. When His own hands brought His own life a victim to the altar-cross, all 'typical' functions were fulfilled. But now on heaven's throne He ministers. There He presents the ever-fragrant incense of His blood. There He portions out the covenanted mercies. Thence freely He outpours them. He came--He lived--He worked--He died, that He might bless. He gave Himself--the price of blessings. He rose--He took His seat on high, that He might reign a Priest, forever blessed, and forever blessing.

Is there a child of Adam's needy race, who covets blessings from the courts of heaven? Let him approach. There is one open way. No fiery sword drives from it. No--a gracious hand is ever beckoning--and gracious invitations call. Hasten to Christ. He is the home of blessings.

Do any ask, When did Aaron's sons thus bless the people? On what occasion were these sounds proclaimed? The Spirit gives not a distinct reply. It is conjectured, that when the morning lamb was offered, the happy worshipers were thus dismissed. If so, when they drew near to gaze on emblems of the dying Lord, these notes hymned peace round their departing steps. It is ever true, that no poor sinner can look up to Christ, without receiving harvests of delight. Who can approach, and not retire with overflowing cup?

If the foregoing thought be right, the sons of Israel once only in each day rejoiced in this blessing. It only fell as morning-manna. But now, around the Gospel-camp, the sound unceasingly is heard. There is no moment, when the believer may not be thus cheered. Christ--his Priest--is always near. In every place--in every work--he may realize His voice, and hear the constant music of the mighty blessing, "The Lord bless you, and keep you; the Lord make His face to shine upon you, and be gracious unto you; the Lord lift up His countenance upon you, and give you peace." The heavenly voice is never mute. The heavenly sun knows no eclipse.

Next, the **terms** are aptly chosen to solace individual hearts. Observe--these blessings are not given, as a general store. They are not cast, as handfuls to a crowd--where some may gather much, and some return with none. Far otherwise. They single out each separate child of faith. They call each one alone, and say, Here is a blessing for your own bosom-need. Each one, apart from all his fellows, takes for himself a full supply.

These lineaments pervade our Gospel. It proclaims special grace. It brings home direct comfort to each soul. The true believer comes apart from men; he leaves the maze of general mercies; he feels, Christ "loved me, and gave Himself for me," as if redemption centered all in me. He lives in heaven, and prays at God's right hand, and fits a bright throne, *for me*, as if I were His only care. I see my own name foremost on His breast. To me the words come especially, "The Lord bless you and keep you; the Lord make His face shine upon you, and be gracious unto you; the Lord lift up His countenance upon you and give you peace."

But if there be this special mercy in the singular address, is there not threefold mercy in the triple voice? With tender love Jehovah is thrice named. Blessings are multiplied--again--again--again. Faith quickly grasps the significance. Three glorious persons form the glorious Godhead. Doubtless they are one in undivided essence--one in coequal majesty--one in the singleness of unchangeable decree--one in the boundlessness of love--one in the exercise of might--one in accomplishment of plan. But there is Trinity in this mystic Unity. One Deity is three in office.

But the whole heart of the Triune Jehovah yearns over the redeemed. They all concur to save. They all combine to help. They all unite to bless. Surely the Threefold Blessing sounds this truth.

Heed--heed again the heaven-sent form. "The Lord," Jehovah the Father, "bless you and keep you." Again--"The Lord," Jehovah the Son, "make His face shine upon you, and be gracious unto you." Again--"The Lord," Jehovah the Holy Spirit, "lift up His countenance upon you, and give you peace."

Our souls are now prepared to press the juice of these rich clusters.

1. Open the hand wide. The **FATHER** comes to fill it. "The Lord bless you, and keep you." The first word is large, as God is large. It gives so much, that it leaves nothing ungiven. It floods the cup, so that no other drop can enter. It shows a prospect, in which there is no vacancy. "The Lord bless you." May He, who speaks, and it is done; who wills, and it must be; who holds all power in His hands; who sits on the high throne of universal rule, may He bless you!

WHEN? Now and ever--throughout the moments, which are and shall be--when you go out--come in--sit down--rise up--through all your living space, and when the last breath flutters on your lips.--"The Lord bless you."

WHERE? In every place, in which you tarry, or to which you move; in the closet--at home--abroad--in still retreat, and in the busiest haunts--in the publicity of open work--and in the sanctity of holiest spots.--"The Lord bless you."

HOW? By causing all things to minister to your true good--by crowning your lot with all real happiness.--"The Lord bless you."

Perhaps the soul, conscious of weakness, finding SELF to be a broken reed, and seeing many perils all around, sighs specially for protection. Be it so. Protection here is stretched out, as a shield--help is extended, as a sustaining arm. It is added, "and keep you." From WHAT? From every foe's injurious assault--from every secret dart--from every direct attack--from self--from men--from evil's legion--from the world's smile and frown. HOW? By the shelter of His shadowing wings. HOW LONG? Until all need is past, and danger's region is quite left behind, and heaven's safe haven is attained. Happy believer--thus blest--thus kept of God!

2. **JESUS** comes next. "The Lord make His face shine upon you, and be gracious unto you." The greatest change on nature's brow is when light dawns. Gloom dwells beneath the pall of night. When clouds cast their thick shade, dark chilliness prevails. But with returning beams the landscape sparkles, the groves are melody, the fields are joy. It is so with the soul. *Sad are the hours, which are not bright with Jesus.* Then sins affright, and wrath dismays, and all the future is despair. There is no misery like the absence of His look. But when His face again is seen, the heart is happiness, the lips are praise. This blessing promises the shining of His face--not a brief ray, but the full blaze of concentrated love. Heaven's fullness is to see Him face to face. Heaven's foretaste, is to catch this pledge of His smile. "The Lord make His face shine upon you."

Here, too, a precious pearl is added. It is GRACE. The words proceed, "and be gracious unto you." What wonders are wrapped up in grace! Its birth is in the heavens--its fruit upon the earth. It looks on those, in whom no merit dwells. It sees them lost. But still it loves, and pities, and relieves. It drew salvation's scheme. It named salvation's sons. It raised the cross, and led the Savior to it. Apart from Christ--it has no being--and no admission-door to its beloved work. But now, through Christ, its visits come on sanctifying wing. The graceless become gracious, because grace *works.* The gracious become glorious, because grace *triumphs.*

3. The blessing voice still speaks. "The Lord lift up His countenance upon you, and give you peace." Can they, who have received so much, need more? But more is wondrously given. The truly blest have all the blessings of a Triune Jehovah. Hence the **SPIRIT'S** favor is moreover pledged. Some covet earthly honors and applause. Some seek the bursting coffer and the large estate. But what is earth, and all its contents, compared to this possession? The Spirit's countenance converts the soul from death to life, and raises it from hell to glory. He shows its utter need, and its recovery in Christ. He teaches the vile loathsomeness of sin--and the just punishment of hell. He then reveals the God-man slain--the shelter of His wounds--the mantle of His righteousness. He points to welcoming arms. He testifies, that none can perish at the cross. When He lifts up His countenance, the mists of ignorance, the clouds of unbelief, melt off--and SELF is seen, that it may be

abhorred--and Christ is seen, that He may be embraced and loved. Then peace will surely follow. There is no peace in soul-blindness, in distance from Christ, in unsubdued iniquity, in wallowing in nature's mire. But when the Spirit joins the soul to Christ--when He renews the nature, and sows seeds of godliness; then peace--abundant peace--peace always, by all means, establishes glad sway.

Reader, seek Christ--adhere to Him--abide in Him--make Him your all--then will this Threefold Blessing be your crown. Hear it once more. "The Lord bless you, and keep you; the Lord make His face shine upon you, and be gracious unto you; the Lord lift up His countenance upon you, and give you peace."

It is the gift of gifts--the prize of prizes--the Father's full protection--the Savior's smiling grace--the Spirit's countenance and peace. Reader, do you ask, Can such transcendent property be mine? Pause--think. Why is it thus revealed? God speaks these blessings, not to mock, but to fulfill. Can they be mine? Oh! cast yourself without one fear on Christ, and you will quickly know.

THE SILVER TRUMPETS

"Make two Trumpets of Silver." Numb. 10:2.

Sinai's ordinances here end. The hallowed mount must now be left. But before the onward-signal sounds, God speaks again. A final token testifies, that Israel's every matter occupies His heart.

A mandate issues to form Trumpets. In number they are two. Their metal is pure silver. As in the golden candlestick, each is constructed from one piece. There is no joint--no link--no mixture. The priests alone may use them. Their purpose is fourfold.

1. Their liquid note convenes assemblies to the tabernacle-door.

2. They sound, when the moving pillar calls the tribes to march (verse 2).

3. They warn, when hostile armies threaten battle (verse 9).

4. On festive days they peal melodiously around the blood-stained altar. Such are these Trumpets--such their use. Each order is divine.

Reader, this is our grace-day. We live, that we may glean soul-profit. The Bible is our harvest field. Here this ordinance now meets us, and offers no small riches to our store.

An obvious thought stands on the threshold. We see God's all-pervading care. He directs all things for His people's welfare. Their least arrangements are arranged in heaven.

How happy; then, is the child of faith! The grand concerns of his eternal home are firmly settled. The door is opened--the passport is provided--fit robes are wrought, by the God-man's redeeming work. A new heart, fit for pure joys, is created by the Spirit. But this is not all. Heavenly plans are not restricted to these heavenly things. *Each little matter on the earthly stage is offspring of decree.* The countless links in each day's chain are framed above. The way, then, must be right, because divinely marked. Chance guides no vessel through life's waves.

Reader, hence learn to scorn no matter, as too small for thought. There are no trifles in a soul's career. *Minute things* sometimes seems to turn the scale for heaven or hell. Make conscience of each trivial event. It has an influence on eternity. When God appears to order two Silver Trumpets for the camp, surely He stamps all little things with magnitude.

The MATERIAL must be silver. This is a metal carefully prepared. Repeated fires cleanse it from all dross. Hence it is emblem of rare purity. "The words of the Lord are pure words--as silver tried in a furnace of earth, purified seven times." Ps. 12:6. Each vessel in the camp of God must be thus clean. "Holiness becomes Your house, O Lord, forever." Ps. 93:5. Ministers should precede with silver-brightness. The flock should follow, as silver without alloy.

Let us now draw nearer to the camp. Two priests are seen. Each blows a Silver Trumpet. Light falls hence on *the office of God's ministers*. Their voice should sound with trumpet-clearness through the flock. They are entrusted with God's message to a fallen world. Theirs is the privilege to tell the story of redeeming grace. They bear grand tidings, which are life to the dead--health to the sick--liberty to the captive--joy to the mourner--comfort to the broken-hearted--wealth to the poor--sight to the blind--recovery to the lost--strength to the weak. As heralds, they have to announce, that God is reconciled--a ransom found--a remedy provided--a Savior given--a Deliverer sent. It is their work to cry, Behold the cross--look to the dying Lamb--flee to His sheltering arms--hide in His wounded side--nestle beneath the covert of His wings--put on the glories of His righteousness--trust in His finished work--plead His atoning sacrifice--present by faith His wrath-appeasing death--receive Him, as all wisdom, joy, and peace--cling to Him through life, in death, forever--in answer to all Satan's wiles, and conscience-fears, shout, 'Christ is All'. They have to warn of the world's murderous arts--of sin's tremendous doom--of fire, which is never quenched--of anguish, which exceeds all thought--of an eternity in darkness and despair.

Should they not, then, with clarion-shrillness, rouse the flock? The Silver Trumpets sent a PIERCING note. So should the Gospel-herald utter aloud the Gospel-news. Away with timid whisper--and a stammering tongue. The servant's lips should glory in the Master's name. Let statements be unmistakable, as the sun without one cloud–clear, as the crystal stream--distinct, as the unmuffled trumpet's voice.

Note, the Trumpets were of ONE PIECE. So is the Gospel-message. It knows no mixture. It is no piece-meal fabric. It is not partly grace and partly works. It calls not men to finish what the Lord commenced. From first to last--in origin--in progress--in conclusion--Gospel-salvation is a free gift. All merit is in Christ. He opens heaven. He closes hell. He washes, decks, and fits. He presents His children pure and faultless. Their pardon and their fitness is

His work. They follow Him, because He calls. They love, because He wins their hearts. They conquer, because He is their sword and shield. They persevere, because His hand upholds. Their grace is offspring of His love. Their glory is the payment of His worth. Thus Christ is All. No diverse metal soiled these Trumpets. No intermingling error should soil pulpits.

The type, moreover, fixes attention on the Christian as a worshiper--a pilgrim--a warrior--a son of joy. For let the OCCASIONS, on which these Trumpets sounded, be now more closely marked.

1. The call the people to God's sanctuary. Reader, mark this. It is a Gospel-ordinance, that worshipers should throng the holy courts--that public prayer and praise should reverence the glorious name. Who will not hasten to obey? Who will not join the people, who keep holy-day? A saintly congregation is an foretaste of heaven. It is earth's holiest scene. What sanctity pervades the spot! What blessedness inspires the company! The Triune God is mighty in the midst. The SPIRIT intercedes within the soul. He prompts longing desires. He makes sin's burden to be felt. He deepens penitential grief. He fans the flame of wrestling supplication. He brightens the torch of love. The GREAT HIGH-PRIEST draws near. He takes each prayer, and washes it in cleansing blood. He perfumes every note of praise. He then presents the fragrant sacrifice before the throne. The FATHER is well-pleased. The service is accepted. Pardons are sealed. Blessings fly down. The faithful meet to honor God. They honor and are honored. They come in faith, and they depart in peace.

Reader, do not think, say not, that such assemblage is superfluous. Doubtless God is not linked to means. He can bless in solitude, and hear in the secluded closet. But it has pleased Him to order public worship. His commands are always gain. The pious congregation thrives. Faith hears--obeys--and finds obedience to be wealth.

2. The trumpets give command to march. Christians are portion of a *marching* host. The Bible warns, that earth is not our rest. We live a stranger-life. We occupy a moving tent. We hold a pilgrim-staff. What is there stationary here? Our days are a fast-flowing stream. The rapid current rushes onward. Let then no heart cast anchor on these sands. Let not affection entwine its fibers around earthly stems. Our mansions are on high. Our home is far away. Be prepared for the journey. Let all be ready for departure. Death should not find a Christian unequipped for march. It is a friend, for whom expecting eyes should watch. The ears should listen for the chariot-wheels. When it appears, let there be no tremor--no surprise--no work unfinished. The Gospel's Silver Trumpets ever cry, 'Arise, Depart. Come up here'.

3. The trumpets sound for war. The life of faith is one incessant fight. Beneath the cross, a sword is drawn, of which the scabbard is cast far away. The attitude of bold defiance is assumed. Until the victor's crown is won, unflinching combat must go on. The foes are many--mighty--wily--restless. They meet us, at each step. They lurk in every corner. They infest our public walk. They enter our closed doors. They are without--around--within. Count, if you can, the hateful legions, who compose hell's hosts--they all rush at the soul. Survey the world--its snares--its foul seductions--its enticing arts--its siren calls--its smiles--its venom-sneers--its terrifying threats. Each in its turn assails--and each, when foiled, renews the assault. Behold the heart, and all its brood of lusts and raging passions. How often it betrays! How often it beguiles! The Gospel-trumpet ever cries, 'Battle is near. Stand firm. Resist'.

But when the Gospel calls, it promises sure triumph. It gives an armor, wrought by God. This, rightly used, cannot be broken. It points to a Captain, by whose side no battle can be lost--beneath whose banner, no warrior was ever slain.

Believer, hear, and go forth in hope. Face all your foes. Grasp manfully your sword. Use skillfully your shield. Lift up the head, safe in salvation's helmet. Shout boldly your great Leader's name. The fight will soon be over. The victor's song will soon be on your lips.

4. They have a further use. **In the grand feasts the trumpets cheer the worshipers around the bleeding victims.** While the altar streams, and happy crowds look on, the heavens resound with these exulting melodies. The precept is obeyed, "Sing aloud unto God our strength--make a joyful noise unto the God of Jacob." Ps. 81:1.

Believer, thus, too, the Gospel teaches you to rejoice--to rejoice with heart abounding with melodious praise, when you in faith contemplate, and in worship plead, the meritorious death of Christ.

My soul, obey, remember Calvary, and sing--shout--pour forth music of delight. Let all, that is within you, swell the adoring chorus. Gaze on the cross--and let exulting hallelujahs testify, how fervently you love--how rapturously you extol--how undoubtingly you trust, that *death*, which is your life--that *blood*, which is your ransom--those *wounds*, which are your shelter--that *Jesus*, who is your full salvation--that *Christ*, who is your All.

Reader, the Gospel-trumpet is now within your hearing. But it is prelude of another melody. Yet a little while, and "the Lord Himself shall descend from heaven with a shout--with the voice of the Archangel and the trumpet of God." 1 Thess. 4:16. That note will open every grave, and wake the sleeping dust, and gather mankind to the great white throne. Quickly you will hear it--for every ear shall hear. It introduces the coronation-day of saints. It is the knell of execution to the lost. Are you prepared? Do you stand ready--one with Christ? If you heed now the Gospel-trumpet calling you to Him, you will hear then the last-day-trumpet calling you to glory.

It is faith's happiest hour, when it goes forth in spirit to intermingle in the fast-coming scene. "We shall not all sleep, but we shall all be changed, in a moment, in the twinkling of an eye, at the last Trumpet--for the Trumpet shall sound, and the dead shall be raised incorruptible, and we shall be changed. For this corruptible must put on incorruption, and this mortal must put on immortality. Then shall be brought to pass the saying, that is written, "Death is swallowed up in victory. O death, where is your sting? O grave, where is your victory?" 1 Cor. 15:51-55.

My soul, hark! hark! This Trumpet soon will sound. Bless Jesus--and fear not.

THE INVITATION

"One day Moses said to his brother-in-law, Hobab son of Reuel the Midianite, We are journeying unto the place, of which the Lord said, I will give it to you--come with us, and we will do you good--for the Lord has spoken good concerning Israel." Numb. 10:29.

Israel's sojourn round the mount is over. The pillar is about to wave its beckoning hand. The silver trumpets are prepared to sound. The happy tribes are ready for the march. Soon all will be an onward progress toward the promised land.

The sight strongly arrests a Christian heart. Who can survey it, and not cry--'Blessed are those who follow a preceding God! Father, lead me, guide me, keep me to the end!'

At this moment the eye of Moses turns with tender yearning to his kinsman Hobab. He for a while had been the comrade of these tribes. Thus he had learned, that they were God's peculiar care. The mighty proofs of present Deity were all familiar to his mind. But outward evidence alone conveys not inward grace. He is not fixed. His feelings fluctuate. He hesitates. He casts a lingering look towards the attractions of an early home. The former ties retain their hold. The well-known scenes allure him back. Like Lot's wife, his eyes look back. While Israel girds the pilgrim-garb, he deliberates on going back.

Moses well knew, that to return was wreck of soul. It is no gain to move from God. There is no profit in forbidden paths. Happiness departs, when God is left. All earth is but a barren waste, without the dew of grace. All is a void, unless God smiles and fills.

Moses had the experience of the better choice. He scorned the courtly pomp. He had trampled on all Egypt's treasures. He had embraced affliction with God's people. And he had found God's favor to be wealth of wealth--the joy of joys.

Reader, make God your own, and you have all. To barter Him for lower things, is to clasp a shadow--snatch a husk--pursue a mocking candle--lean on a broken reed. There is no poverty like a worldling's lot. What is a crown upon a godless head? What is a scepter in a graceless hand? What is all gold to an impoverished soul? What were the plains of Sodom to ease-seeking Lot? Had Lazarus or Dives the happier heart?

Moses beholds the doubting Hobab. He pities--and he sincerely would win him to a wiser choice. Therefore he thus tenderly expostulates. *"We are journeying to the Promised Land. Come with us and we will do you good, for the Lord has promised good things to Israel!"*

He states the fact. We are indeed a moving camp. Our rest is yet far off. But we advance not as uncertainly. We follow no deceiving guide. There is a home conspicuously bright in view. It glitters in the rays of heavenly pledge. God's love, and word, and power, secure it.

And then he pressingly invites, *"Come with us."* Turn not away. Recede not to a heathen land. Join not again the people, whose home is darkness--whose walk is misery--whose end is woe. But cleave to us. All good is then your portion. We move not blindly. God's voice is gone forth, strewing blessings round us. Goodness and mercy from His courts walk, as companions, by our side. He dwells in us. We dwell in Him. Come then, come then with us.

So Moses reasoned--so he called.

1. His invitation shows **FAITH'S HAPPY STATE**. It is a mirror reflecting the features of calm trust. Full faith has eagle-eye. It penetrates all earthly mists. It gazes steadily on Zion's highest light. It is content to live a stranger-life on earth. It would not settle in this thorny nest. It would not lie down beside such poison-streams. This climate is too cheerless. It looks aloft. Its true affections center round a purer scene. So daily it moves forward. And nightly realizes, that an upward step is made. We are journeying unto the promised place.

What is this place? Faith gazes--it ever gazes with increasing rapture--but it fails fully to describe.

It is **rest**. The happy inhabitants go no more put. No further step is needed. No loftier summit can be scaled. The pilgrim lays aside his staff, and sits down in undisturbed delight. The warrior's wounds are healed. His struggles and his conflicts cease. The watch-tower is exchanged for sure repose. The sword has found its sheath. The shield wearies the arm no more. No foe can enter into victory's domain. Reader, do you not long to reach it?

It is perfect **purity**. Earth's misery is sin. Saints groan, because they so often stumble. The constant struggle and the frequent fall cause anguish. The flesh is weak. Temptations fiercely and most craftily assail. The garments contract stains. But in this place sin cannot come. The tempter is barred out. No step again can be unclean. No thought again can go astray. Heaven would not be welcome to a new-born man, unless it were one flood of godlike purity. Reader, do you not long to reach it?

It is **joy**. Where sin is absent, peace must reign. Where God is present, happiness must overflow. Heaven is a boundless ocean, in which each swelling wave is pleasure in the highest. It is a prospect ever widening, in which each scene is rapturous delight. It is skies, forever brightening, in which each orb is sparkling ecstasy. It must be so--for love is the one pulse in every heart--praise is the endless sound from every lip--hallelujah the one ceaseless echo. The blessed cannot cease to sing, because fresh views of their thrice-blessed state continually arise. It must be so--for they behold the glories of their Lord--not in dim distance--not through the varying medium of faith--but near, and never to depart--but clear, and ever clearer. Transporting joy! daily to read new glories in the face of Christ--daily to dive into the deep wonders of the love of God. Reader, do not you long to be there?

Faith holds the title-deeds of this celestial mansion. The word is spoken. "I will give it to you." It is a gift--and a gift worthy of the God, who gives--worthy of the blood, which bought--worthy of the Spirit, who calls to it. No human merit pays the price. No human strength can scale the steps. No human hand opens the gate. Some proudly hope for heaven, as if they had some claim. But none go proudly in. They all fall low before the throne, shouting glory to free grace--Salvation to the Lamb--"Christ is All."

But it is sure. "I will give it to you." **Who** utters this wondrous promise? Even the Lord, whose might is almightiness--before whom all men, and all the hosts of hell, are nothing, and far less. Let every foe swell into millions of ten millions--let all their power be thousand-fold increased--His arm can shiver them to dust-- His breath can drive them, as a feather on the hurricane's wing. The Lord, whose word is truth--whose counsels are immutability--whose purpose ever stands--says, "I will give it to you." Faith hears and knows, that every wave and every gale convey it prosperously to the assured haven. "We are journeying unto a place, of which the Lord said, I will give it to you--come with us." Such is faith's happy state. Reader, have you this faith?

2. This invitation shows, that **FAITH IS AGGRESSIVE**. "Come with us." Each heaven-set plant strives for expanse. True grace has one sure sign--it longs and labors to communicate its wealth. A saving view of Christ slays self--relaxes every icy band--widely extends embracing arms, and yearns to multiply delights. When the heart burns, the life must labor. Where is the fire, which emits

no warmth? Where is the sun, which darts forth no rays? Thus the history of faith is *a chart of plans and toils for Christ.*

It looks around. It first marks the Hobabs of the home-circle. It stops not here. It takes a wider prospect. It surveys the neighboring abodes. It then mounts higher ground, and flies around the circumference of the native land. It still ascends, and in the telescopic gaze of love, it comprehends the world, with its broad circuit, and all its mass of people--kindred--tongues.

While it thus muses, what is the deep desire? Oh! that these souls might be the heirs of heavenly life! Their nature-state dooms them indeed to wrath. Their steps unturned must bear them down to hell. Their hearts unchanged must link them to the lost. But Jesus died, and in that death there is redemption. But Jesus lives, and while He lives, who can despair? If only they can hear of Him--if the sweet mercies of the Spirit help--if faith convey them to the cross--then soul-graves open--then endless misery flees, as night before the orb of day--then hell is robbed, and angels shout.

While faith thus pants with longing hopes, it asks, 'How shall this be?' The answer is at hand. God tells what aid must be employed. The means are the clear proclamation of the Gospel-truth. And this proclamation is from preachers' lips. Then preachers must be sent forth. The men of God, with Christ on their lips--the Bible in their hands--must take their stand between the living and the dead. They must lift high the Gospel-beacon amid a lost world's night. Rejoicing in their known salvation, they must importunately urge, "We are journeying unto the place, of which the Lord said, I will give it to you--come with us, land we will do you good."

Faith then will hasten to give far-flying wings to these appointed means. This holy zeal became the parent of missions to home-destitute, and distant heathen. Hence arose that precious brotherhood of combined believers, who send salvation's tidings far and near. But how scanty are their efforts before a world's need! How crippled are the sinews of their strength! How poor their coffers! How few their laborers!

Reader, are you the called of Christ? Are you a traveler to the promised place? Then show it by your self-denying support to these enlisting laborers. Help them, for they need it. Help them, for the time is short. Help them, for the Lord requires it. Help them, as you would have sure token in the day of Christ, that you obeyed His mandate, and that your faith was not a barren stock.

But perhaps some Hobab reads these lines, who is not pressing on to Zion's joys. Sir, pause and reflect. This tract, with Moses-like entreaty, grasps your hand, and looks you tenderly in the face, and knocks imploringly at your heart's door. It asks with loving zeal, Where do your footsteps tend? It prays you to turn and join yourself in heavenly fellowship to heaven-bound travelers. "Come with us."

Your present path is misery--briers--thorns--rough places--pit-falls--disappointments, all sloping towards hell. Before us there is peace, and an eternity of light. Turn, "come with us." The world, and sin, and Satan, pierce with death-wounds. But "we will do you good." Behold the Savior, whom we love, and trust, and serve. Can you depart from Him? Oh! mark His tender grace--His zeal for souls--His surety-sufferings--His guilt-expiating agony. Can you leave Him? Think of His patience--His frequent calls--His precious promises--His outstretched arms. Think of the rapture of His seen smile--the comfort of His felt presence--the calm delights of converse with Him, and the full glories of His near kingdom. Think of the dying Lamb--the risen Lord--the reigning and triumphant King. "Come with us." Jesus has spoken good concerning Israel.

May the mighty Spirit prompt the quick reply, 'Grace conquers, and I come!' May hesitation hide its face in shame! May wise decision make you Christ's forever.

THE RISING AND THE RESTING PRAYER

"It came to pass, when the ark set forward, that Moses said, Rise up, Lord, and let Your enemies be scattered; and let those who hate You, flee before You--And when it rested, he said, Return, O Lord, unto the many thousands of Israel." Numb. 10:35, 36.

When the ark moves, a praying voice is heard. When the tribes halt, and tents receive them, again it sounds. Prayer consecrates the going forth and coming in. It opens the door for departure. It bolts the resting-place. It is the vanguard to precede. It is the rear-guard to lock in. It sanctifies the extreme links--and so the entire chain.

My soul, often view this teaching fact. Moses begins and ends with hands--with eyes--with heart--uplifted. The first--the last look, is towards heaven. He seeks a journeying blessing, before he stirs. He asks resting blessing, when he rests.

This is true wisdom and real grace. Happy the life, which is one flow of prayer! It is the pilgrim's staff--the warrior's sword--the pillow of the weary--the refuge of distress--the cry, which proves the man to be new-born. It is the wing, on which the soul flies upward. It is the tongue, which asks--the hand, which takes--great things. It has free access to a mercy-seat, and there it carries on a gainful trade.

Believer, to you each day is a new journey. Each circumstance is an onward step. Each morning calls you to a march. Each night is as the spreading of a resting tent. Each finished work is as another pause in your advancing pilgrimage. Let then your progress be one stream of supplication. None ever prayed enough. Many in life and death bewail soul-poverty. The cause is poverty of prayer. Much is badly done--much is undone--because prayer is not well-done. What scales can weigh the profit, which might thus be earned! What thought can estimate the loss, which prayerless hours incur!

"Rise up, Lord." "Return, O Lord." Such is the Rising and the Resting Prayer. There is strong significance in the petitions. They are as arrows wisely pointed to a mark. They breathe a definite design. They are not weak in vagueness of unmeaning generality.

Some prayers are forms, in which no feature is exact. The words are many, but clear thought is rare. But true grace always realizes *need*. And then distinctly seeks *relief*. It asks with known and felt intent.

Let, now, the substance of these prayers be sifted.

1. THE RISING PRAYER. "Rise up, Lord, and let Your enemies be scattered--and let those who hate You, flee before You." Here is confession, that Israel's onward path was thronged with foes. It is so still, and so will always be. Opposing armies are in front. Each step must be through hostile ranks. The rest is reached through many a fight. The Canaanite--the Amorite--the myriads of Satan's seed--still live. They leave no stratagem untried--no weapon unemployed. There is no hour, when sword and shield may hang unused.

Next Moses feels, that his own might is nothing--vain are his counsels--powerless is his arm. When not upheld, he falls. Unaided, he is driven back. His hope--his trust--his strength--his armor--his success--his triumph--are from God. Therefore to God he flees. "Rise up, Lord." So now, if God's right hand be not our help, the tide of foes must bear us down. But God is moved by importunities of faith. "Rise up, Lord," is a cry, which brings all heaven to aid. It puts sure victory on the wing.

Observe here, how the prayer of faith yearns for God's glory. "Let *Your* enemies be scattered." These enemies hate God. They would impede the progress of His truth. They would extinguish His word's light. They would cast down His righteous rule. Can faith sit still and see Him thus dethroned? Oh! no. It agonizes with desire, that He would vindicate His holy cause--uphold His honor, and add trophies to His name. "Rise up, Lord, and let those who hate You, flee before You."

Believer, act out this pattern. Be zealous for God's kingdom. Let every thought center in Him. Strive that He may increase. Let Him be magnified--exalted--glorified--and then care not, that SELF lies low.

Realize, too, your oneness with the Lord. His life is your life. His death is your death. His resurrection is your revival. In Him you died, and rose, and sit now at God's right hand. So, too, His cause, His foes, are yours; and yours are His. Thus, when temptations fiercely try, you may appeal to Him, These are Your conflicts--"Rise up, Lord." These weapons seek Your injury--"Rise up, Lord, and let Your enemies be scattered--and let those who hate You, flee before You."

2. THE RESTING-PRAYER. "Return, O Lord, to the many thousands of Israel." The going forth would have been ruin, except the Lord moved in the front. The rest will be no rest, unless the Lord return. Prayer called Him to precede their steps. Prayer calls Him to abide around their resting tents. Vast was the multitude. But what are numbers without God? His presence is their power--their peace--their joy--their glory--their strength--their fortress--their shield, and their repose. They know it, and they cry, "Return, O Lord."

Reader, what is your home--what is your heart--if God be absent? That family alone is blessed, in which God has His constant seat. The table is a sweet feast, when He presides. The home circle beams with pure delights, when He is seen in every smiling look. The house is sheltered, when His wings spread the canopy around.

But is God willing to abide with men? His word expels all doubt. The promises hang in clusters. "Draw near to God, and He will draw near to you." Jam. 4:8. Do you ask, 'But how can one so vile, so base--so hateful through iniquity--so stained with sin's polluting filth--draw near to one so holy and so high?' A ready path is open. Christ is the way. Flee to His arms, and you reach God. In Christ distance is swallowed up--and union is cemented.

Hear next Christ's sweet assurance. "If a man loves me, he will keep my words--and my Father will love him, and we will come unto him, and make our abode with him." John 14:23. Give then your heart to Christ. Make His commands your constant walk. And then you are the temple of His presence. He will come in, and with Him all the glories of indwelling Deity.

Heed, too, the wondrous word, "Thus says the high and lofty One, who inhabits eternity, whose name is Holy--I dwell in the high and holy place, with him also that is of a contrite and humble spirit." Is. 57:15. Then ask the Spirit to lead you along humility's low valley. God will meet you there, and make your heart His home. Thus you may be filled with all the fullness of your God-- your soul may be a present heaven--your eye may ever rest upon His smile--your ear may ever hear the whispers of His love. At the close of every hour--duty--conflict, pray with undoubting faith, "Return, O Lord," and surely God will come.

We are next taught, that these petitions have enduring life. They are a model to the end of time. Let none suppose, that, when the ark crossed Jordan, they were cast aside. No rather, they flow on a never-failing stream. They blossom, as an over-verdant tree. Let David give the proof. When ages had flown by, he brought the ark, with joyful pomp, to Zion's hill. Where shall his heart find fitting praise? These words supply it. "Let God arise, let His enemies be scattered--let them also, who hate Him flee before Him." Ps. 68:1. My soul, may you, too, ever use this Prayer--at all times fit!

But these high words from David's lips open a more glorious view. When he thus sings beside the ark, he has an onward look to Christ. He sees redemption's Lord riding in redemption's chariot. He lauds Him, as the mighty conqueror traveling in triumph's pomp. Else, why should he add, "You have ascended on high--You have led captivity captive--You have received gifts for men, yes, for the rebellious also, that the Lord God might dwell among them?" Ps. 68:18. You have done gloriously, as salvation's captain. All your foes, where are they? They have fled. They are all scattered, as the dust before the wind.

Thus the **Rising** and the Resting Prayer beside the rising and the resting ark lead us directly to our conquering and our coming Jesus. Faith claps the hand, and sings aloud, 'Here is my Lord'.

Yes. The moving ark is type of Jesus going forth to cast down rebel foes. It is high joy to trace the Antitype's victorious march. How mightily the Lord advanced! The strength of God was in His arm. His sword was Deity. His darts were barbed with all Jehovah's might. "He had on His vesture and on His thigh a name written, King of kings, and Lord of lords." Rev. 19:16. His foes, indeed, strove mightily. It was no easy work, to rescue souls from Satan's grasp--or to lay low the prison-house of darkness. The enemy rushed on, clad in his fiercest armor--wild in his keenest rage--wily in his deadliest crafts. He plied His every temptation, as a terrific battery. But the true Ark never quailed. The adversary licked the dust. Malignant passions maddened in opposing breasts. The kings stood up--rulers took counsel--all plots were laid--the ignominious death was planned and executed. But still the Ark moved on. The cross gave aid--not injury. The grave could not detain. Death could not vanquish. The gates of hell fly open. The mighty conqueror appears. And as in Canaan, the ark ascended Zion's hill amid triumphant shouts, so Jesus mounts on high. The heaven of heavens receives Him. The Father welcomes the all-conquering Savior. Angelic hosts adore the glorious God-man. The Rising Prayer has full accomplishment, "Rise up, Lord, and let Your enemies be scattered, and let those who hate You flee before You."

And now from glory's throne He cheers His humble followers in their desert-march. Their toils, their conflicts, and their fears are many. They ofttimes seem, as a poor worm beneath the crushing feet. But they survive--they prosper--they lift up the head. As of old the ark was victory--so Jesus is victory now. Yes--every child of faith shall surely set a conquering foot upon the host of foes. Hear this, you mad opposers, and desist. Where are the nations, who resisted Israel? Where are the Pharaohs--the beleaguered kings-- the Herods--the chief-priests--the Pilates? Share not their malice, lest you share their end. Read in this word your near destruction, "Rise up, Lord, and let Your enemies be scattered, and let those who hate You flee before You."

And as the Rising Prayer has never failed, so, too, the **Resting Prayer** now teems with life. "Return, O Lord." Jesus is ready to fly back. Israel's many thousands wait, but wait not in vain. "Yet a little while, and He who shall come will come, and will not tarry." Heb. 10:37. Oh! joyful day--triumphant sight! What ecstasy--what shouts--what glory! Salvation's Lord returns. Welcome--welcome to Him!

Reader, what will be your state on that bright morn? Will your lips shout, "This is the Lord, we have waited for Him?" What is the answer of your heart? Is it now swelling with the cry, "Come, Lord Jesus, come quickly?"--"Return, O Lord, to, the many thousands of Israel."

This is the grand event, for which the earth now sighs. And will it tarry long? Scripture has long since said, "The coming of the Lord draws near." "The Judge stands before the door." Jam. 5:8. Believer, be wise. Be looking from your watch-tower. Are there no rays streaking the horizon? Extend the listening ear. Is there no sound of chariot-wheels in startling events?

GRAPES OF ESHCOL

"When they came to what is now known as the valley of Eshcol, they cut down a cluster of grapes so large that it took two of them to carry it on a pole between them!" Numbers 13:23

"They came unto the brook of Eshcol, and cut down from thence a branch with one cluster of grapes." Numb. 13:23.

We reach the valley of Eshcol through a humbling path. Before we touch its clustering grapes, let the dark steps be traced. The story shows, how vile is man--and how gracious is our God! It proves our proneness to transgress. It then presents an emblem of the heavenly bliss.

When Sinai is left, the march of Israel advances prosperously. There is no check. No enemy annoys. No difficulties hinder. Each day the intervening wilderness decreases; and the desired land is neared. And now the very borders are in view. A few more steps will plant the pilgrim-host in Canaan.

Surely courage will now brace each nerve--joy will beat high in every heart--and with triumphant praise they will plant conquering banners. But is it so? Alas! they pause--they hesitate. Jehovah's ancient covenant fades from their view. The pledged support--the daily help--the experienced favor--are forgotten, as an unsubstantial dream. The unworthy thought creeps in--perchance the nations are too strong for us--their walled cities, and their iron gates may beat back our assault.

Thus they distrust--and tremblingly propose to search the country by spies. They take weak counsel with their carnal minds. They follow sight--not faith. They cast behind their backs the oath to Abraham--the repeated promise to their fathers--and the rich map of the luxuriant plains, so often drawn by God's describing hand.

Such are the workings of *vile unbelief.* And that dark monster is not dead. Yet--yet it lives. It lurks in corners of each heart. It ever watches to bring its disguise to every eye--its poison-draught to every lip. It is crafty to whisper, that perhaps God's many promises may fail; that faith may be pursuing a vain shadow; and may lie down at last misled--deceived--undone.

Reader, beware--look inward. If you discern the slightest trace of this beguiling serpent, oh! spare it not--seize it and slay it on the

altar of revealed truth. Take for the solid pavement of your steps,
"It is written." Then manfully advance. Grasp tight the promises;
and boldly march toward your pledged inheritance. Let nothing
tempt you to test heaven's counsels at the bar of human sense.
He is the fool of fools, who tests divine assurances in the scales of
mortal vision.

But this timid policy befools Israel's camp. The spies are named.
They are sent forth to ascertain, whether their God be true. They
pass from place to place. They view the mountains and the valleys.
Then in their progress they reach Eshcol's brook. Here fruit before
unknown for size, for beauty, and for luxuriant juice, meets their
admiring gaze. They pluck one cluster from the vine. The treasure
needs two men to bear it. Upon a staff they prop it up. And thus
they seek the camp, laden with a trophy of the country's wealth.

Here let the spies be left. Here let a curtain fall on their sad errand and their sin. Their sin--for they bring back a false report-
-and while they show the fruit, they largely dwell upon the walled
towns, and monster-forms, and other formidable sights. But from
such conduct let us turn. It is more solacing to contemplate that
cluster, which they bear--that earnest of rich fields.

The Spirit teaching, we may draw hence a foretaste of the full
riches of our celestial land. These grapes are proof of Canaan's
exuberant fertility. The giant-produce testifies abundance. So, too,
there is **a heavenly Eshcol** before faith's eye. It shows delicious
clusters. And should we not delight to walk in the enchanting
ground, and cheer our spirits with the glowing prospect? Surely Eshcol's luxuriance portrays our glorious Canaan. It pictures
heaven--our looked-for rest--the mark, to which we press--the haven of our storm-tossed voyage--the end of weary pilgrimage--the
soul's eternal home--the land of every delight. This Eshcol should
be ever in our view.

The joy before Christ cheered His heart. The joy before us should
gird up our loins. The racer bounds, when he discerns the goal in
sight. The mariner is alert, when land is seen. The soul spreads
swifter wings, when heaven seems to open.

Reader, come, then, in Eshcol's grapes, read *faith's amazing
prize*.

But here thought flags--mind fails--all words seem emptiness-
-all images fall short. No angel's tongue can adequately paint the
brightness of those realms. Mortal powers shrink into very noth-
ingness. None can describe heaven, but those who enter it. And
those who enter it, find their delight an ever-swelling flood--an

ever-brightening day--an ever-opening flower--a volume, which eternity cannot read through!

Heaven! It is the palace of the great Eternal. Salvation is its walls--its gates are praise. Its pavement is purity's most golden luster. Its atmosphere is perfect love. Heaven! It is the home prepared by God before the worlds were made, for His redeemed children. It is the mansion, which the ascended Jesus still labors to make fit. Heaven! It is so attractive, that all Jehovah's skill cannot increase the beauty--so full, that nothing can be added--so rich, that it can hold no more.

But Eshcol's luxuriance allures us to more close examination. Let us draw nearer. This cluster was the vine's perfection. So, too, perfection is the essence of our heaven. Nothing can enter there to stain--to soil--to vex--to humble. Oh! what a contrast to our present state! We would be holy--but, alas! a treacherous adversary rolls us in the mire. Our hearts are daily pierced. We loathe and we abhor ourselves. But our high home is barricaded against sin. Never--never--never--can iniquity again intrude. The soul forever joys--righteous, as God is righteous--pure, as God is pure. Reader, seek heaven. But heaven is more than this.

Here on earth, the **foul tempter** all day long is spreading nets. There is no saint too saintly for his vile approach. In Eden he approached the innocent. To Jesus he said, 'Worship me'. His whispers, his bold lies, as keenest anguish, haunt the regenerate heart. And while life lasts, there is no respite. He watches every dying bed. But in heaven this misery has ceased. *No serpent crawls along that pavement!* Satan is outside--far off--the bottomless pit has shut its mouth upon him. Reader, seek heaven. But heaven is more than this.

Here on earth, **fears** rush in. The ground is slippery. A precipice is near. We tremble on the brink. Fiery darts fly round. We shudder, lest some poison penetrate our veins. The torturing thought breaks in, 'Will my frail bark hold out! Will even God's own grace endure my daily provocations! May I not, after all, fail of salvation! May not my end be with the lost!' But fear dies at heaven's gate! The happy company realize, that they are lofty above injury. Their throne is safety in the highest. They know it--what then can they fear? Reader, seek heaven. But heaven is more than this.

Earth is **affliction's** home. A troop of sorrows compass us about. Tears stream. The bosom sighs. The brow is furrowed by the lines of care and worry. Death tears away the much-loved friend. Sickness invades the frame. The home is desolate. The table is destitute. We look to the right-hand, and there is trouble--on the left, and still fresh troubles frown. But heaven is a wide sea of bliss without a ripple. All tears are wiped away. All faces beam with one enraptured smile. All lips confess, 'The cup of happiness overflows'. We bathe in oceans of delight. Reader, seek heaven. But heaven is more than this.

Here **unbelief** often gathers, as a chilly cloud. It mantles the soul in darkness. It suggests apprehension, that His love has ceased, and that desertion is, or may be, our lot. This is a miserable condition. When God is felt to be a God at hand, woe ceases to be woe, and burdens are all light. But in heaven a present God is always everywhere. *We cannot move beyond the sunshine of His love.* His countenance is universal brightness. Reader, seek heaven. But heaven is more than this.

Here **ignorance** leads us in a floundering path. We thirst for knowledge, but we reach it not. How much concerning God is utterly beyond our grasp! Blindness curtails our perspective. Clouds narrow our view. But heaven is a realm without horizon. We know God, as we are known. We love intelligently. We understand, whom we adore. Reader, seek heaven. But heaven is more than this.

Sin is shut out--temptations banished--fears buried in an unfathomable grave--sorrow and unbelief have fled away--knowledge is perfect--our souls are purity--our bodies are imperishable beauty--we completely share the glory of our all-glorious Lord. How much is this! But yet this is not all.

In the true Eshcol's cluster there is this richer fruit--Jesus is seen. This is the crown of heaven. This is the pinnacle of bliss. The rising of the sun makes day. The presence of the king constitutes the court. The revelation of the Lord, without one intervening cloud, is the grand glory of the endless kingdom. Heaven is full heaven, because Christ shines there exactly as He is--seen and admired of every eye.

Faith searches for Him now in types, and shadows, and prophetic forms, and sacraments, and holy emblems. This sight is precious--gratefully to be enjoyed--devoutly to be improved. But these are faint outlines of the eternal vision. These often are obscured. But in heaven Jesus ever stands conspicuous in one undiminishable blaze.

Believer, what will it be to gaze on the manifested beauty of Him, who is so altogether lovely! What! to read clearly all the deep mysteries of His redeeming will! What! to dive down to the vast depths of His unfathomable heart! What! to fly upward to the very sum-

mit of His boundless love! What! to trace clearly all His dealings
in providence and grace! What! to comprehend all that Jesus is!
What! never to lose sight of Him--no, not for a moment! What! to
be ever drinking fresh raptures from His present smile! What! to
feel, that this joy is mine forever! What! to shout, 'Come on, you
ages of eternity, you never part me from my Lord!' This--this is
heaven. This--this is Eshcol's full cluster.

Reader, are you a traveler towards this heaven? When you behold the grapes of Eshcol, do you know, that the vineyard is your
sure heritage? The question may be solved. This kingdom is for
the subjects of the King--this palace is for His sons. Are you, then,
His by faith? They, who are in Him now, will dwell with Him forever. They, who live Christ on earth, go to Him in the upper world.
Then ask, "Is your soul knit to Him? Are you a branch engrafted
in the heavenly stem? Are you the bride espoused to the Lamb?"
Conscience well knows.

The link, which thus connects, is faith. This is that precious
grace, which sees His worth--flees to Him--embraces Him--and
holds Him tight. This is that heaven-given power, which, with glad
hand, receives the title-deeds of heaven. This is that Spirit-im-
planted confidence, which looks to Eshcol, and claims all Canaan,
as a promised home.

Reader, never rest, then, until, standing on firm Gospel-ground,
you can look up and cry, "Lord, I believe." Then daily feed on Eshcol's grapes. Then daily move towards Canaan. You soon will hear,
"Come you blessed of my Father, inherit the kingdom prepared for
you from the foundation of the world." Matt. 25:34.

THE BUDDED ROD

"The next day Moses entered the Tent of the Testimony and saw that Aaron's staff, which represented the house of Levi, had not only sprouted but had budded, blossomed and produced almonds."
Numbers 17:8

A new miracle now meets us. It is God's work. It is the Spirit's record. Therefore it stands here for our souls' profit. A withered rod, long severed from the parent stem, in which all vital juice was dried, sprouts in fresh verdure. Buds show their infant forms, and clustering blossoms open, while fruit in ripe luxuriance hangs.

This fact claims special thought, from its position in the sacred page. It raises a conspicuous head high in a vast field of miracle. Israel's whole journey is a chain of marvels. The falling manna--the guiding cloud--the flowing stream--prove heavenly care. Each day evidences, that omnipotence is active for them. But here a fresh prodigy starts to life. God superadds another sign to win confiding trust.

To us this story of the Budded Rod now comes. May He, who wrought the wonder, work wonders through it for our growth in grace!

But before we view it with a nearer eye, we must not disregard the preceding notes. The faithless spies draw an appalling picture of the searched land. The fortresses defy assault. The men are giants. Israel's hosts are less than insects at their feet. Such is their evil record. And it is received. Hearts quake. Blaspheming tongues reproach their guiding God.

Thus nature shows its proneness to doubt, to tremble, and to distrust. But such UNBELIEF brings misery in its train. It is a seed, from which ill ever springs. It changes blessings into curse. It arms the hand of love with an avenging scourge.

So now wrath instantly goes forth. The murmuring hosts are doomed to turn their back upon the home just reached. The wilderness must be re-entered. They now must wander up and down for forty years. Thus their bright prospects end in darkest night. Their hopes of rest--almost attained--are gone. They must wear out in woe their dismal days.

Distrust! truly you are the parent of all woe! My soul, never distrust--cleave fast to God--cast deep your anchor in His word--bear all things--suffer all pains--but never let one rebel doubt arise.

Pause now, and pray, "O Spirit of the living God, never withdraw--leave me not to the fears, which sense and folly would excite. Lord, I believe; help my unbelief."

Surely the downcast host will now tread tremblingly their retrogressing path--their lips will now be sad with penitence and shame. They, who so reason, are yet blind to the deep roots of sin. *As there is no mercy, which man's heart will not abuse, so there is no judgment, which it will not proudly scorn.* Open rebellion soon follows these murmurs and this punishment. Korah and his company dispute the rule of Moses. They challenge it, as usurpation and self-arrogance. Thus God's authority is dethroned. But these leaders are leading at His call. Therefore, to revile them is to revile His will.

Instantly terrific vengeance vindicates God's ways. Moses proclaims the near approach of impending wrath; and, "He had hardly finished speaking the words when the ground suddenly split open beneath them. The earth opened up and swallowed the men, along with their households and the followers who were standing with them, and everything they owned. So they went down alive into the grave, along with their belongings. The earth closed over them, and they all vanished." Numbers 16:31-33

Again we are disposed to cry, 'surely now rebellion must be buried in that grave! Surely obedience now will meekly walk with God!' But we soon find, that *sin has seeds so deep*, and fibers so far-spreading, that while most withering judgments are descending, it still will germinate and bring forth its weeds.

The morrow dawns, but not to see contrition in each face. No, rather, it finds one flood of universal rage. The camp is indignant against the servants of the Lord. The whole assembly raises the cry, "You have killed the people of the Lord," But sin cannot thus sin, and wrath not multiply to punish. A slaying plague speeds forth. It rapidly mows down the God-defying host. Moses beseeches Aaron to rush forth. He grasps his censer--fills it with incense--adds the altar-fire--and takes his station between the living and the dead. God sees the mediating high-priest–the type of His dear Son. The sight checks wrath. But still a plague-struck pile stands, as a mighty pyramid--a monument of sin's deserts.

Now, at this moment, God gives the miracle of the Budded Rod. Another sign now shames unbelieving doubts, and pictures Gospel-truth. The people had scorned Aaron's priestly rights. God's overflowing love selects this very time to add confirmation of His choice. Twelve rods are taken. Each bears the name of the chief ruler of a tribe. They are deposited before the ark. Thus the night passes. When the morrow comes, Moses re-enters. Eleven lie, as they were placed, withered, lifeless, dry. The twelfth, engraved with Aaron's name, is changed--most marvelously changed! Verdure adorns it--but not verdure only. No branch was ever so enriched. Blossoms are joined to buds. And amid blossoms ripe fruits swell. Man's hand has no share here. The proof of God's immediate power appears in every part. The rod, thus vivified, is to be kept a constant sign. God's voice commands, "Bring Aaron's rod again before the testimony, to be kept for a sign against the rebels." Numb. 17:10.

Let us now advance from the ancient record, to the still-living Gospel of the fact. The Rod in many graphic tints shows Jesus. The very name is caught by raptured prophets. Hark, how they announce Him. "There shall come forth a *Rod* out of the stem of Jesse, and a Branch shall grow out of his roots." Is. 11:1. "Behold the man, whose name is The *Branch*; and He shall grow up out of His place, and He shall build the temple of the Lord--and He shall bear the glory, and shall sit and rule upon His throne--and He shall be a Priest upon His throne." Zech. 6:12, 13. Thus faith gleans lessons from the very title--Rod.

But the grand significance of the type is to REJECT ALL RIVALS. It sets Aaron alone upon the priestly seat. The parallel proclaims, that similarly *JESUS is our only Priest.* God calls--anoints--appoints--accepts, and ever hears Him--but Him alone. In His hands only do these functions live. He sprinkles the true mercy-seat with ever-pleading blood. He bears His people's name upon His breast. He perfumes all their petitions--praises--service, with meritorious fragrance. He intercedes, and they are pardoned. He blesses, and all blessings crown them. But He shares not the glory with a colleague. They, who seek God with *censers of their own,* like Korah scorn the only avenue--like Korah rush to ruin. My soul, be satisfied with Jesus. Shout--"None but the consecrated God-man--He is my total Priest--I need no more."

Next, the constant luxuriance has a clear voice. In nature's field, buds--blossoms--fruit, soon wither. The grove--the garden--lovely in spring--laden in autumn--soon droop. Not so this Rod. Its rich abundance was forever rich. Its verdure was forever green. Its fruit was ever ripe. Beside the ark it was reserved in never-fading beauty. Here is the ever-blooming Priesthood of our Lord. "You

are a Priest forever, after the order of Melchizedek." Ps. 110:4.
"This man--because He continues forever--has an unchangeable
Priesthood." Heb. 7:24. What joy--what rapture fills the heart of
faith, when with adoring eye it looks aloft and sees its ever-living
High-Priest on the throne! At every moment Jesus stands in all the
freshness of salvation's vigor. Our prayers are ofttimes cold and
languid. Our lips are dull to speak. Our thoughts stray far away.
Petitions are as an intermitting stream. The channel sometimes
is quite dry. It is not so in heaven. There, always is full tide of
priestly mediation. Here is the cause why saints prevail, and grace
survives. Hence Satan with all his legioned host is beaten back.
Hence faith's tiny bark rides on the crest of mountain-waves, and
safely reaches the blest haven. Hence plans for Gospel-progress
triumph. Because Christ ever lives, and ever loves, and ever prays,
and ever works, therefore His kingdom swells.

And so it shall be, while the need remains. But when the last of
the redeemed is safely gathered in, then heaven shall no more hear
the interceding Priest. Then the one sound from the vast throng
shall be--Hallelujah. Thus the Rod, ever fresh--shows Jesus ever
mighty in His Priestly power.

Mark, moreover, that types of Jesus often comprehend the
CHURCH. It is so with these rods. The twelve rods at first seem all
alike. They are all sapless twigs. The same grove saw their birth.
Man's eye sees but one likeness in their dry forms. But suddenly
one puts forth loveliness--while the others still remain worthless
and withered. Here is a picture of God's dealings with a sin-slain
race. Since Adam's fall, all are born lifeless branches of a withered stock. Many abide so, and thus pass as fuel to the quenchless fire. But in a chosen remnant, a new birth occurs. The grave
sprouts into life. The sapless put forth buds. Blossoms appear.
Fruit ripens. Whence is the difference? It is not nature's work.
No dry stick can restore itself. No withered helplessness can deck
itself with verdure. This cannot be. When any child of man arises
from the death of sin, and blooms in grace, God has arisen with
divine almightiness. Free, sovereign love decrees renewal. Boundless power achieves it.

Believer, the Budded Rod gives another warning. It is a picture
of LUXURIANCE. Turn from it and look inward. Is your soul thus
richly fertile? Is life in you abundant life? *Where are the almonds?*
They are rare. Instead of fruit, you often yield the thorn. Should it
be so? "Herein is My Father glorified, that you bear much fruit, so
shall you be My disciples." John 15:8. Whence is the fault? Why is

the stem thus bare? The fertilizing means abound. Perhaps they are little heeded. "Abide in Me and I in you--as the branch cannot bear fruit of itself, except it abide in the vine, no more can you, except you abide in Me." John 15:4. Perhaps your neglectful soul departs from Christ. Thus fructifying sap is checked. Thus bloom is nipped. Thus early buds fall off. You leave the sunny slopes of Zion's hill. You stray into the chilly marshes of the world. Then blight and mildew mar the expected fruit. The Word is not the daily food. Hence the roots drink not renovating moisture--and the withered leaf drops off. Meditate in God's law day and night, and you "shall be like a tree planted by the rivers of waters, that brings forth his *fruit* in his season--his leaf also shall not wither--and whatever he does shall *prosper.*" Ps. 1:3.

But if the Budded Rod rebukes the scanty fruit in the newborn soul, what is its voice to unregenerate worldlings? Alas! these are a forest of sticks, wholly dry. The curse, which fell on Eden's garden, blasted their nature to the core. Thus withered they were born. Thus withered they continue. What will their end be? That end draws near. What then awaits them? Can they be beams and rafters in the palace of heaven's King! Oh! no. The decree is sure. Faithfulness has warned. Almighty power will execute. "That, which bears thorns and briers, is rejected, and is near unto cursing, whose end is to be burned." Heb. 6:8.

THE RED HEIFER

"Tell the Israelites to bring you a **red heifer** *without defect or blemish and that has never been under a yoke."* Numbers 19:2

Contact with death is the occasion of this type.

DEATH! The very sound falls heavily. What mind can lightly think of it? What eye unmoved can see it? The limbs, once full of vigor, stir no more. Sinews, once elastic in activity, become rigid. The form, so wondrous in its mechanism, becomes an inert mass. The features, once the reflecting mirror of ten thousand thoughts, are marble-monotony. The vessel, once so proudly merry, lies a deserted wreck. The fabric, once so sparkling in beauty, is a deserted ruin.

Death! It is more than animation fled. Decay draws near, with a polluting touch. Corruption fastens on its prey. The friends, most dotingly attached, cannot but turn loathingly away. A stern necessity requires, that offensive remains be buried out of sight.

Reader, here pause and meditate. This death is pressing at your heels. It soon will lay you low. Your weeping friends will hide you in the dust. A forgetting world will go on merrily, as though you had not been. Say, do you joyfully await its touch? Can you feel, Death comes as with friendly hand to open the cage-door, that my freed spirit may fly to its high home? Remember, you cannot escape. This tyrant wields a universal sway.

But in what cradle is it born? Whence is it armed with that destroying scythe? It is transgression's child. Sin is the womb which bore it. A sinless world would have been deathless bloom. But the world is sinful, and therefore is an open tomb.

In Eden sin was foreseen, and therefore death was fore-announced. Obey and live--but disobey, and "you shall surely die." Gen. 2:17. The miserable sequel is well known. The tempter came. The bold lie triumphed. And from that day our fallen earth has been one charnel-house.

Hence death is no ingredient in creation's primal law. It is a shadow cast by a blighted ruin. In its features we read wrath--displeasure--curse. Its voice is sternly one--God is offended. Its scourge vindicates eternal majesty and truth.

Death, then, is perpetual evidence, that rebellion has worked extensively. It follows, because sin has preceded. Now God, in love, desires to set this truth conspicuously before each eye. Hence He writes a clear decree in Israel's code. "Whoever touches a dead body, is unclean seven days." Numb. 19:11. The man, thus soiled, is outcast from the tabernacle-service. He is exiled from social fellowships. The rule is universal. "This is the ritual law that applies when someone dies in a tent: Those who enter that tent, and those who were inside when the death occurred, will be ceremonially unclean for seven days. Any container in the tent that was not covered with a lid is also defiled. And if someone outdoors touches the corpse of someone who was killed with a sword or who died a natural death, or if someone touches a human bone or a grave, that person will be unclean for seven days." Numbers 19:14-16

This is a rigid law. But it speaks clearly. How awfully it shows *God's sense of sin!* Whoever is brought near to *death*--sin's symbol--is symbolically vile. Proximity to *lifelessness*--sin's work--is counted, as proximity to sin itself. The contact with the sign, is branded, as contact with the thing signified.

But pollution may thus occur, which no forethought could flee. Without intent the foot might touch a grave. In ignorance a tent might be entered, where death sat. The decent *offices of love* might require, that lifeless relatives be carried out. Care must hide those, who cannot hide themselves. Be it so. It matters not what be the cause--if death is touched, legal uncleanness is incurred.

We hence are taught, *how sin surrounds us, and how suddenly it soils*. It is the very atmosphere of earth. Man cannot move, but some contamination meets him. His casual walk is along *miry* paths. In the discharge of *pious* duties some *stain* may soon defile. Thus each day's course may render us impure.

This is a humbling truth. But in this very darkness there is light. We are not left bereft of remedy. The unclean may be cleansed. All stains may vanish. There is a fountain opened for all soul-filth. There is full help for foulest need. Where sin abounds, sin's cure exceeds. Where pollution spreads its wide pall, the Savior brings His wider covering. This is the Gospel-message. And this stands prominently forth in the provision for removing the defilement of death's touch.

Reader, come view now the ordinance of the Red Heifer. And while you view, bless God for the great antitype--Christ Jesus.

God, who sentences the unclean, appears now to relieve. No remedy could be devised by man. None could be credited, unless it brings heaven's seal. Faith cannot rest, but on a God-erected rock. But He provides, and He reveals. *"Tell the Israelites to bring you a **red heifer** without defect or blemish and that has never been under a yoke."* Numbers 19:2.

In the first place THE VICTIM IS SPECIFIED. But still the people must present it. Thus Christ, God's sacrifice for sin, is taken from earth's sons. That it may be so, He puts on our nature. He clothes Himself with humanity, as the Woman's Seed. So our race is enabled to give from its fold the sin-removing offering. The pitying angels could not find this help. Their nature is distinct from ours. Their glittering hosts hold not a substitute for man. The children of Israel must bring a Red Heifer.

The HEIFER'S COLOR is precisely fixed. It must be **red** throughout, without one spot. Faith learns most precious lessons from this rule. What is Adam, but red earth? Hence, then, the ruddy type manifests our Lord, as Adam's offering. Yes, He is truly man, that He may take man's place, and bear man's guilt--and pay man's curse--and suffer in man's stead. The Heifer--RED--proclaims, that in nature Christ is verily what Adam was--sin always excepted--and verily what Adam's children are. Believer, rejoice. As man, you sinned--as man, you merit hell--but Christ has lived, and worked, and died, a God-man in your stead.

But Scripture-types have many phases. PURE RED recalls the thought of **blood**. And can faith look to Jesus and not mark His streaming wounds? He stands in vesture dipped in blood. He shed it, and thus satisfies for sin. He shows it by the Spirit to the soul, and thus infuses peace. He pleads it before God, and thus obtains the blessings, which His Cross bought.

"WITHOUT DEFECT OR BLEMISH." The Heifer must be perfect. This is a general requisition. Completeness must adorn each victim on God's altar. The slightest blemish was exclusion. This always shows our Jesus--spotless in perfection's brightest luster. Truly He was man, but truly He was man immeasurably far from sin. From the first breath, until His return in triumph to His throne, He was as clean from evil, as Jehovah in the highest. No sunbeam is more clear from darkness, than Jesus from sin's shadow. If it could have been otherwise, how could He have atoned for us? Sin's touch would have made Him subservient to justice. Death would have been due for His own faults. But now He gives His soul--His body--without one blemish, a pure--fit--all-sufficient sacrifice for all the sins of His most sinful flock. Such is the lesson from the Heifer without blemish.

THE NECK ALSO MUST BE UNMARKED BY YOKE. It never may

have yielded to compulsion's lash. It must be unused to *imposed work*. Thus Jesus bounds with willing step to Calvary, "Lo I come." Constraint compelled Him not. No force reluctantly dragged Him. His moving impulse was pure love--love for His Father's name--love for immortal souls--love springing fresh from the deep fountains of His heart--love, as free as the air.

Christ is all willingness. Who can be tardy, when He calls? Christ flies on rapid wings to save. Who will not fly on rapid wing towards Him?

The Heifer is then dragged outside the camp. As a vile thing it is cast out. The dwelling place of man rejects it. The type is answered, when Jesus, reviled--despised--spit on--mangled--scorned, is led beyond the city's gates. Ignominy's cup then over flows. He is reproached, as vilest refuse.

Believer, do not expect favor with the world. They, who scorned Jesus, will not honor you. Submit with His most lamb-like patience. Follow Him amid all sneers. Endure the *cross*. It raises to a *crown*.

Next it is SLAIN. And did not Jesus die? He did, for death was our desert. Therefore, He drank that cup. What grace what love! what glorious rescue! what complete redemption! what full atonement! In very deed the God-man dies. Believer, clasp the truth--exult--adore. When sins reproach--when conscience stings--when Satan rages--when the white throne is set, shout, "Christ died!" This answers every charge--silences each adversary's voice--breaks Satan's chains--quenches hell's flames--tears out the worm's sting--annihilates destruction--brings in salvation. The truth, that Jesus died, is glory to God--glory for man--glory forever!

The Priest then turns towards the Mercy-seat, and seven times SPRINKLES THE BLOOD. The Gospel-story is replete with blood. We here again are taught its triumphs. It opens the door to the pure sanctuary above. It clears the way. None enter, but along this consecrated path. This sprinkling is the only key.

FIRE IS THEN APPLIED, and the whole Heifer is *consumed*. The *unsparing element* devours all, and soon reduces it to ashes. We see in this, how *vengeance deals relentlessly with our sin-laden Surety*. It only checks its hand, when no more can be taken. Sweet are the tidings, that no wrath remains for those, who die in Christ. Their agony is past--their punishment is paid--all now before them is eternity of love.

Finally, THE ASHES ARE COLLECTED. Mingled with water from a running stream, they form a purifying store. This is laid up for those polluted by the touch of death. Through seven days such must be counted, as unclean. Upon the third and seventh, they are sprinkled by a hyssop-rod dipped in this fluid. And then impurity departs. Then the excluding taint is cleansed away.

Thus ends the rite. But Gospel truth still lives in the eternal record. A fundamental truth is prominent. As these ashes purify the ceremonially impure--so virtue from the dying cross takes moral guilt away.

But we learn more. The ashes are not used alone. They are commingled with PURE WATER. This sparkling produce of the spring portrays the **Spirit's grace**. Hence, though Christ's death obliterates *condemnatory* stains, the Spirit must come in with further aid, to wash the heart, and fit it for heavenly home. This hallowed fluid is applied by a hyssop-bunch. This rod is emblem of the faith, which ventures near, and claims the merit of redemption's store, and then applies it to the soul. Ashes unsprinkled availed not. The Gospel-hope ungrasped is worth nothing. Faith's hand must clasp and use it.

Reader, is there not here most large instruction for your soul? Each day sees you unclean. Say, is your faith each day most closely dealing with the Savior's death, and with the Spirit's love? In the Red Heifer you are taught the remedy prepared by God. He hates, indeed, the filth of sin, But He provides--proclaims--extends full expiation. All is now ready to make you whiter than the whitest snow. Come, then, draw near in faith. Be clean--be sanctified--be saved.

THE BRAZEN SERPENT

*"The Lord said unto Moses, Make a **fiery serpent**, and set it upon a pole--and it shall come to pass that everyone who is bitten, when he looks upon it shall live. So Moses made a **serpent** out of **bronze** and attached it to the top of a pole. Whenever those who were bitten looked at the bronze snake, they recovered!"* Numbers 21:8-9

Alas! what broods of vileness nestle in man's heart! As wave succeeds to wave, sin presses on the heels of sin. If a brief calm seems to give peace, a fiercer storm soon rises. The seeds of evil, for a while concealed, revive as weeds in spring. All human history proves this. But the recurring murmurs in the wilderness are saddest evidence. Seven times already has rebellion raged. And now again, because the way is long, there is revolt, and blasphemies are muttered, "and they began to murmur against God and Moses. 'Why have you brought us out of Egypt to die here in the wilderness?' they complained. 'There is nothing to eat here and nothing to drink. And we hate this wretched manna!'" Numbers 21:5

Here is another proof, that *there is no blindness like UNBELIEF.* Surely the sweetest manna fell with every morning's dawn. Surely the purest stream flowed closely in their rear. But harsh ingratitude sees frowns on mercy's loveliest brow. Reader, are not your features in this picture? By nature this same quarry is your cradle. You spring, a branch of this sin-bearing tree. And if fretful distrust be not your constant fruit, free grace has wrought in you a mighty change.

Israel's murmurs soon plunge them into deep waters of distress. Hence learn to dread this evil. Flee its touch. Bar fast the door against its entrance. Wrath follows in its rear. The dregs of woe are in its cup. Whoever sinned and suffered not? See what swift vengeance overtakes these rebels! "The Lord sent *fiery serpents* among the people, and they bit the people--and many people of Israel died." Numb. 21:6.

The camp is now wide-spread dismay. These *messengers of wrath* beset each path. No care can flee them. Their dart is sudden. Their sting is death. Thus multitudes sink tortured to the grave.

But Israel's sin gives opportunity for grace to smile. Mercy often uses punishment, as a cure. A scourge is sent to check the downward course. How many find recovery in *suffering's valley!* How many rise, because they were cast down! A rod is often evidence of love. It is so here. The stricken crowds now feel their guilt. Self-loathingly they mourn. They beseech Moses, "Pray unto the Lord, that He take away the serpents from us."

Moses complies. He here appears a type of his forgiving--mediating--Lord. He gives no railing for their cruel taunts. He upbraids them not for unbelief. He reminds them not, that this misery was the due wages of their ways. He quickly flies to God. Can prayer knock earnestly at heaven's gate and be unheeded? Eternal truth proclaims, "Ask, and you shall have." Christian experience responds, "This poor man cried, and the Lord heard him, and saved him out of all his troubles." Ps. 34:6. Rejoicing multitudes have proved--are proving--that *faithful petition prospers.* Its gains are ever sure and large. When supplication wrestles, plenteous showers of grace are on the wing.

But it is mercy's way, to give more than our hearts expect. Behold a proof. The people seek a respite from the plague. This would, indeed, have been a gracious boon. But it would have left *the bitten* to expire. It would, indeed, have checked the flowing tide of fiery ill. But it would not have eased the pain-racked limb. And what is more, it would have reared no Gospel-beacon for all ages of the Church. But the reply exceeds requests. It thus is worthy of a giving God. It is an ocean of vast love. It is a volume of deep wisdom. It is a flower redolent of saving truth. God takes occasion from this sin to cheer souls to the end of time. "The Lord said unto Moses, Make a fiery serpent, and set it upon a pole--and it shall come to pass, that every one that is bitten, when he looks upon it shall live." Numb. 21:8.

Relief for body is conceded. But, so marvelous is the plan, that human skill is silent in amaze. No mind could have conceived such mode. Indeed, proud reason would assuredly despise it. But cure for body is the smallest portion of this mercy. It shows the cross, in form too clear for doubts--in colors, which no age can fade.

It is instructive to observe, how Moses staggers not here in unbelief. God speaks. That is enough. Therefore the plan is wise--therefore it must succeed. So, instantly he executes. "He made a serpent of brass, and put it upon a pole--and it came to pass, that if a serpent had bitten any man, when he beheld the serpent of brass, he lived." Numb. 21:9.

Behold God's method--simple, yet mighty; one only, yet sufficient for each case. The prince, the poor, must seek the selfsame remedy. The mightiest intellect--the most expanded mind--the most inventive thought--could find no other rescue. The most illiterate had instant access to it. The aged raised the eye, and health returned. The youthful gazed, and malady was gone. In some, the pains were great, and death seemed near, but *one view killed the plague.* Others had just felt the sting, and found the pain to fly. Some were far off in distant borders of the camp--some had their dwellings around the uplifted pole--but every look--from far--from near--was full, complete, and instantaneous cure.

Did any scorn the means? If so, neglect was ruin. No other help could heal the bite. But all, who acted trust in God's appointed mode, found sure deliverance. There was only one remedy--free--open unto all--but only one. Look, and be healed. Look, and let life return.

The glory of this type now gloriously breaks. Let minor thoughts now vanish, as stars before the sun. **The Brazen Serpent on the pole is Christ.** The look towards it is faith. This must be granted. The lips, which cannot err--which cannot lead astray--decide. When Jesus opened wisdom's volume to Nicodemus, He brought him to this very scene. The words are as bright as midday. "As Moses lifted up the serpent in the wilderness, even so must the Son of Man be lifted up--that whoever believes in Him, should not perish, but have eternal life." John 3:14, 15.

Blessed record! sweet sound! amazing truth! grand tidings worth ten thousand worlds! Here then, in emblem, is *the gospel of free grace!* Here is the remedy of God. Here is relief commensurate with all the need of all poor sin-sick souls. Reader, give ear. See in this figure your hope--your joy--your peace--your full redemption--your complete salvation--your curse removed--your sins all blotted out! Come, and look **in**ward--realize your neediness--your pain--your rankling sore--your just exposure to eternal death. And then look **up**ward and behold health in a bleeding Savior's wounds--life in a dying Savior's death.

Mark, PERISHING is no fable's vain conceit. These words warn of it, "that whoever believes in Him should not perish." The bitten sufferer truly pictures our very case. We too are pilgrims journeying through a wild wilderness. It is infested with the old serpent and his brood. At every step, at every turn, we meet some forked attack. Each day the mischief taints our veins. Satan's least touch is fatal venom. In Eden he began his murderous work. And still his fiery darts fly round. No mother's son escapes. All earth is perishing like Israel's camp. But earth brings no relief. If penitence forever wept--if sighs ceased not--if rolling hours were one con- tinued wail--the streaming eye--the smitten breast--the bending knee--the upraised eye--the wringing hand--the supplicating lip could not extract the sting. Self has no help. The Law is no physi- cian. Its glance detects disease. Its voice proclaims the hopeless state. But it holds no cordial remedy in its stores . It denounces the leprous spots. It sternly sentences, and leaves the wounded to expire. Man cannot help himself--or save his brother. No rites--no forms--no services--suck out the poison. As all the sick in Israel's camp were surely lost, unless God had decreed to heal--so all the serpent-wounded upon earth must surely have sunk down to hell, unless free mercy had most freely pitied. But He who said, Raise up a serpent on the pole, said also, Lift up My Son upon the ac- cursed tree.

Thus God resolves to help the helpless--to stay the plague--to save the lost. Praise--praise--His name! Our God is love. Gaze on the proof. He calls His Son to bring relief. Bless--bless His grace! He sends His Jesus from His own bosom to give health!

And can it be, that Jesus refuses to come and deliver us? No, He flies gladly on redeeming wings. He thinks no load too heavy--no agony too great--no ignominy too vile--no shame too shameful, if only He may restore.

My soul, ponder again this healing work. The serpent's sting had slain man's race. The God-man comes to bruise this serpent's head. He, without sin, assumes the form of sinful flesh--and in that form is lifted high up on the cross. He hangs the graphic an- titype of the brass-serpent. He is thus raised up on the cross, that He may be conspicuously displayed to all earth's sons--and that all faithful ministers may learn to lift aloft this only beacon.

Reader, look then from other things towards this cross. Look with assured faith. He, who there hangs, is verily the mighty God. Therefore divinity belongs to those deep wounds. They have in- finity of merit to expiate infinity of guilt. He wears your form--He bears your nature--that His sufferings may be accounted, as your own. In Him all power--all fitness--all sufficiency combine. God sends--accredits--appoints--accepts Him. In Him all attributes are more than satisfied. He is salvation to the uttermost. He is God's glory in the highest.

Look yet more earnestly. The look of faith is saving. You cannot turn a trustful eye to Him and not receive fullest salvation. Did any wounded Israelite look and not live? So no beholding sinner dies. The remedy is sure--is near. You may be **aged**, and long years of sin may show a blackened course. Look, and the mighty mass of sin is gone. You may bewail a life of aggravated guilt. Your stains may be the deepest crimson. You may be plunged and replunged in vilest filth. Look, and be whole. If all the sins of all the lost were yours, they would not exceed this expiating power.

You may be **young**--and life's first buds be opening. But you are born *a withered branch on withered tree. The serpent's poison tainted your infant veins.* You never can have health, but from the cross. The rich must look--for riches cannot save. The *poor* must look--for poverty is no cloak for guilt. The *learned* must look--for learning can devise no other help. The *ignorant* must look--for ignorance is not heaven's key. None ever lived without soul-sickness. None regain strength apart from Christ. But His cross stands uplifted high--even as the pole in Israel's camp. And it is not a vain voice, which cries, "Look unto Me, and be saved, all the ends of the earth!" Is. 45:22.

Believer, you know, that you have **daily** need to look. You are raised high by faith, but not above the *flying* serpent's reach. Alas! how suddenly he wounds God's saints. And all his wounds bring pain. But the reviving cross is ever in sight. There alone, can the venom lose its pain. Then live with your eye riveted on Christ. Thence flow your streams of peace. Turn not away your gaze in life--in death--until you enter the blessed home, where the old serpent cannot come.

JACOB'S STAR
AND ISRAEL'S SCEPTER

*"There shall come a **Star** out of Jacob, and a **Scepter** shall rise out of Israel."* Numb. 24:17.

Jesus is here sweetly preached--but from a heart, which never loved Him, and by lips, which never more shall praise Him. It is indeed an dreadful personage, who now speaks. A cloak of fearful mystery enwraps him. He journeys far to *curse* God's people. But when he comes, he cannot choose but to bless them.

His name is BALAAM. His mind, his motives, and his frightful course, are a deep study. *They are a sign-post, showing hell's downward road.* Thus they present a vast expanse of profit, of which the barest outline only can be touched.

His dwelling was amid the mountains of the East. His intellect had there acquired some knowledge of the living God. His name was wide-spread, as a man enriched with heavenly gifts. He was revered, as having mystic influence in the unseen world.

Hence Balak, Moab's king, dismayed at Israel's conquering course, thinks, that Balaam's aid would avail more than armaments. Therefore he calls him, saying, "I know, that he whom you blessed, is blessed--and he whom you curse, is cursed."

Common reputation thus made him more than man. *But all his outward sanctity concealed a graceless heart.* Disguised in holy livery, he was the slave of this world's prince.

The messengers arrive. Their errand is declared. Balaam's first answer suits his fame. God seems the foremost object of his thoughts. He thus professes, that God's will is his only guide--"Lodge here this night, and I will bring you word again, as the Lord shall speak unto me." And can so fair a morn be soon a rayless night? Alas! a good commencement secures not a good end. The bud may never blossom, and the blossom may not ripen into fruit. *Many a lost one once looked heavenward.*

He tells the matter to his God. The clearest answer is returned. "You shall NOT go with them--you shall not curse the people--for they are blessed." And can it be, that God thus communes with unrighteous men? Yes! Truth may pass the threshold of the mind, and not subdue the heart. Alpine snows reflect the sun, but are not softened by it.

Balaam's half-heartedness now creeps from its disguise. His *ear* received God's plain reply. But his *eye* looked on Balak's rich rewards. He cannot but dismiss the princes. But his weak words betray his hankering heart. He *slightly* says, "The Lord refuses to give me leave to go." Here is not truth in its full stature. The prohibition is withheld--"You shall not curse." The grand decree is cloaked--"For they are blessed."

Unhappy man! one honest speech would have uplifted him above temptation's reach. Alas! for those who halt and linger on the borders of untruth. The timid clippers of God's word, the trembling fritterers, suppress reality, and so deceive.

Satan has cast a wily net. His arts succeed. Balaam told less than God's reply. The princes hasten back, and they tell even less than Balaam's words. Dilution is diluted more. They only say, "Balaam refuses to come." God is now totally left out--and man's demurring will appears the sole hindrance.

The temptation is thus courted to return. And it will not be slow to seek the half-inviting door. Balak sends mightier princes, with larger entreaties, and more costly bribes. Balaam's *mask* now further drops. He frowns them not away. Professing loyalty to God, he urges them to tarry, while he sought further guidance. But he fully knew God's will. Still, regardless of this, a secret longing lurked, that he might get some doubtful word, which seemingly might make compliance guiltless. Alas! for those, who, while they scruple to impinge against a bolted *door*, seek by some *crevice* to get out.

God speaks again; but the restraining rein is slackened. Those who shun light, will soon be left to stumble in the dark. Balaam now only hears, "If the men come to call you, rise up, and go with them." Here is a lowered barrier. And, intent on gain, he quickly overleaps it. Uncalled, he early rises. *And so he rushes down the stream to earthly treasure, and soul-death.*

But now a prodigy bars up his course. The Angel of the Lord thrice stands an adversary in the way; and then "he was rebuked for his wrongdoing by a donkey--a beast without speech--who spoke with a man's voice and restrained the prophet's madness." 2 Peter 2:16. Heaven and earth miraculously restrain him. Still his desire of lucre will not stop. He is surrendered to his evil will. Restraints diminish. He gains the terrible permission to advance. "Go with the men." He deserts God. God deserts him. Thus Balaam reaches

Moab's land. And here he still pretends devotedness to God, while his whole heart worships the idol of cheap reward.

What scenes ensue! Altars are raised. Victims profusely bleed. The king beseeches, tempts, caresses. The wretched prophet struggles to comply. He seeks all means to curse, that so he may grasp the cursed bribe. He mounts the summit of the lofty rock. He thence surveys the outstretched camp. He opens his mouth-- and longs for words to blast God's people, and secure the gold. But all is vain. As a reluctant instrument in mightier hands he cries, "How shall I curse, whom God has not cursed?"

Surely he will now desist. Ah! No. A hateful passion has become his lord. Another vile attempt is made. He moves to Pisgah's heights. Thence but the outskirts of the camp are seen, and there he tarries, courting a seeming license to oppose God without open rejection of a servant's garb. The Lord again distinctly overrules. The struggling traitor cannot but cry, "Behold, I have received commandment to bless--and He has blessed--and I cannot reverse it." Will he not yield to this clear voice! Will he not turn, and rather heap his curses on God's foes!

Ah! what can change the heart, which worldly passions hold in bonds? Once more he seeks an eminence. He fully looks upon the multitudinous company. Again his bad lips open. Again God conquers, and the truth is heard, "Blessed is he, who blesses you, and cursed is he, who curses you."

Do any read, who, against conscience and clear light, would touch forbidden ground? Balaam's case cries, Forbear--forbear! Be firm--be resolute--at once, forever turn away. Dally not with an unholy wish. Now to escape, may not be hard. Tomorrow, resistance weakens, while the lure strengthens.

The prophet vexed--the king enraged, now part. Balak reproaches--Balaam recriminates. They both are foiled. The evil union ends in evil. But Balaam's lips speak once again. Unhappy man! he must proclaim a Savior, in whose salvation he shall have no share.

"I shall see Him, but not now--I shall behold Him, but not near--there shall come a Star out of Jacob, and a Scepter shall rise out of Israel, and shall smite the corners of Moab, and destroy all the children of Sheth." Numb. 24:17.

Thus is the Gospel preached by a dead soul. Let preachers search their inmost hearts. Christ only in the *mind*--the *lips*--the *pulpit*, will not save. Many, many show, who never shall behold, Him. They raise the cross, yet turn away themselves. They praise the blood, yet never wash. They tell of wounds, which they touch not. They open out redemption's scheme, but never clasp redemption's Lord. They teach the truth, and live a lie. They point out the source of life, and pass by it to death. The apostle Judas from the side of Jesus went to his own place. The prophet Balaam thus preached to others, and yet he died the vilest of the vile.

But his clear prophecy now asks attention. Where can more glowing terms of Christ be found? A Star--a Scepter--a two-fold phase of the most glorious sight, which men or angels can behold.

"There shall come a **STAR** out of Jacob." A Star, what is it, but a glittering orb set in the canopy of night? It sparkles, as a gem amid surrounding gloom. It darts a cheering ray on the black pall around. It smiles with lovely radiance on a dark ground.

Such is Christ Jesus. Where He beams not, it is unmitigated night. It is the skies without a star. What is such blackness, but a chilly type of ignorance, and wretchedness, and sin? Take the poor soul, in which Christ never shone. All these vile troops there brood. Is God there known? Far otherwise. There may be vague idea of some supreme director. But the realities of God's grace, and love, and truth, and justice, are utterly unseen. There is no basking in a Father's smile. Each step is through the maze and thickness of impenetrable doubts. There is no joy of a felt pardon. There is no knowledge of sins blotted out. Such is each Christless soul. But let the Star appear--what loveliness pervades the scene! So when Christ rises in the heart, that brightness comes, before which sin and misery flee.

Balaam proclaimed this Star. But his beclouded eye discerned it not. Reader, say, do you see its beauteous light? All, who behold it, reflect its rays.

Next Jesus, who thus enlightens, **exercises sway**. His presence cheers and also subjugates. Another aspect therefore is adjoined. "A **SCEPTER** shall rise out of Israel." These types of Christ may seem most diverse. But they have mystic union. Is not a Savior seen most surely *loved?* Is not a Savior loved most warmly *served?* As surely as we cannot love, until we know; so surely we cannot know and fail to love--so surely we cannot love and not desire to please. Thus the Gospel-beams always give sanctifying warmth. Thus the Star brings a **Scepter** with it.

Experience proves this truth. The holiest man is always he, whose soul is the widest flood of Gospel-light. *The more the Star is seen, the more the Scepter is outstretched.* The more Christ shines within, the more ungodly weeds decline. The Gospel-truth makes all its subjects willing in a day of power. And, when made willing, they no longer live to self, but unto Him, who governs by His love. Balaam proclaimed the Scepter with a rebel-heart. Reader, submit to this most righteous rule.

Mark finally, that Balaam is forced to utter TERROR to a Christ-refusing world. "A **scepter** will rise out of Israel. He will crush the foreheads of Moab, the skulls of all the sons of Sheth." Numbers 24:17. As His willing subjects are exalted, so the rebellious world must perish. They, who submit, are saved. They who resist, are dashed to powder.

Reader, now answer, what is your state? Are you among the happy heirs of this Star's kingdom? If not, take warning. His coming is at hand. His glorious chariot draws near. A blessed gathering throngs it. They sing. They triumph. They give praise. The rebel mass lie prostrate at His feet. The crushing wheels destroy them, and from His presence they are driven to that woe, where no Star rises in the endless night--and the one Scepter is hell's iron sway.

Think, think again of Balaam. He had an inward hell, while yet he lived on earth. Where is there misery like this foresight of woe? "I shall see Him, but not now. I shall behold Him, but not near." His eyes shall see the Lord--too late. Yes. They must open to His glorious view. "But not near!" What! when He calls His ransomed to His side, and bids them occupy His throne, and gaze forever on His beauty, and never leave Him more--what! then to be cast out! Reader, beware! Soon will each doom be fixed!

Phinehas

*The Lord said to Moses, "**Phinehas** son of Eleazar, the son of Aaron, the priest, has turned my anger away from the Israelites; for he was as zealous as I am for my honor among them, so that in my zeal I did not put an end to them. Therefore tell him I am making my covenant of peace with him. He and his descendants will have a covenant of a lasting priesthood, because he was zealous for the honor of his God and made atonement for the Israelites."* Numbers 25:10-13

Phinehas appears, as a rainbow on the bosom of a storm. He is as a flower on a wild heath--a fertile spot in a parched desert--pure gold in a crude quarry--a fragrant rose upon a thorny hedge--faithful among faithless.

The wretched Balaam, held back from cursing, returns not sorrowing to his distant home. He is *restrained,* but not *reformed.* Deep seeds of evil often live, though not permitted to break forth. So it is in him. He lingers still in Moab's godless land. Though often foiled, venom still works within. It seeks an outlet in secret and abominable plots. He counsels Balak to spread lustful lures, and to entice the people to the idol-feast. Let *weapons* be now laid down--*banquets* prepared--and *blandishments* displayed. "Nevertheless, I have a few things against you: You have people there who hold to the teaching of Balaam, who taught Balak to entice the Israelites to sin by eating food sacrificed to idols and by committing sexual immorality." Rev. 2:14.

Ah! what destruction may one bad man cause! One spark may kindle desolating flames. One evil thought may be the seed of many a poison-tree.

Balak adopts the evil plan. The fascinating and enticing net is spread. The people rush in crowds, like fluttering moths to a destroying flame. And thus they fall self-slain. A bosom-traitor yields the fort.

Reader, your greatest danger is from SELF. Bar fast the heart. Chain your own thoughts. Satan's outward malignity may fall innocuous, like Balaam's stifled curse. But, if the heart gives up the door, lusts in vile troops will enter, and do murderous work. How many die--the slaughtered of a yielding will!

While thus the people sin, God's vengeance rises with a giant-arm. Sentence of death is passed upon the guilty. The judges raise the gallows. The offenders perish ignominiously. And, as if executions were too tardy, a pestilence moreover comes, and sweeps its thousands into penal graves.

This is a moment of terrific dread. All sights and sounds of death appear. The frightful scene seems as a picture of the last-day wrath.

Surely now the stoutest heart will quake! Surely one cry for mercy will wail tremblingly in every tent! It is not so. *Judgments, apart from grace, may harden.* The bit may only chafe ungovernable steeds. Thus this appalling moment witnesses the outbreak of increasing sin. Zimri, a prince of loftiest rank, whose station made him the observed of all, dares wrath--sneers at the legal sentence--braves the plague's withering stroke--raises his rebel-hand against all decency and fear, and openly, in plainest vision of the weeping crowds, stalks boldly into sin's embrace. Amid the annals of iniquity, madder contempt of God cannot be found. Sin has sinned vilely, but this is among its most unblushing acts.

Phinehas, the priest, beholds. And zeal for God swells through his soul. He cannot stop the impulse to wipe out the stain. His arm must hasten the just punishment. Thus, with his javelin, he indignantly sweeps hence the titled culprit, and the high-born partner in filth.

So Phinehas felt; and so he acted. What is the result? The Lord gives respite. The plague is stayed. And an approving voice honors the righteous zeal. Behold "I give unto him My covenant of peace--and he shall have it, and his seed after him--even the covenant of an everlasting priesthood."

Reader, now pause, and mark the mighty principle, which rolled like a torrent in the heart of Phinehas. The Spirit leaves it not obscure. The praise is this, "He was zealous for his God." He could not fold his arms, and see God's law insulted--His rule defied--His will despised--His majesty and empire scorned. The servant's heart blazed in one blaze of godly indignation. He must be up to vindicate his Lord. His fervent love--his bold resolve--fear nothing in a righteous cause. The offending Zimri was a potent prince--nevertheless he spared him not.

Believer, can you read this and feel no shame? Do your bold efforts testify your zeal? Sinners blaspheme God's name. Do you rebuke? His Sabbaths are profaned. Do you protest? False principles are current. Do you expose the counterfeits? Vice stalks in virtue's garb. Do you tear down the mask? Satan enthralls the world. Do you resist? No, rather are you not *dozing unconcerned?* Whether Christ's cause succeeds, or be cast down, you little care. If righteous zeal girded your loins, and braced your nerves, and moved the rudder of your heart, and swelled your sails of action, would God be so unknown, and blasphemy so daring?

Mark, next, the zeal of Phinehas is sound-minded. It is not as a horse without rein--a torrent unembanked--a hurricane let loose. Its steps are set in order's path. It executes God's own will in God's own way. The mandate says, let the offenders die. He aims a death-blow, then, with obedient hand. The *zeal*, which heaven kindles, is always a *submissive* grace.

This zeal wrought wonders. It seemed to open heaven's gates for blessings to rush forth. God testifies, "He has turned my wrath away from the children of Israel." He has made atonement for them. My name is rescued from dishonor. The haughty sinner is laid low. Therefore I can restrain my vengeance. Men see, that sin is not unpunished--mercy may now fly righteously to heal.

ZEAL is indeed a wonder-working grace. It scales the heavens in agonizing prayer. It wrestles with omnipotence, and takes not a denial. Who can conceive what countries, districts, cities, families, and men have sprung to life, because zeal prayed? It also lives in energetic toil. It is the moving spring in hearts of apostles, martyrs, reformers, missionaries, and burning preachers of the Word. What hindrances it overleaps! What chains it breaks! What lands it traverses! It encompasses earth with efforts for the truth--and pyramids of saved souls are trophies to its praise. My soul, bestir your every power for Christ. The labor will not be in vain.

Next mark, how heavenly smiles beam on the zeal of Phinehas. Honor decks those, who honor God. The priesthood shall be his. It shall live in his line from age to age. He and his sons shall bear the name of Israel on their breast-plate, and make atonement in the sanctuary. Grand privilege! Such is the fruit of zeal.

Brave works for God win crowns. There is no merit in them. But the grace, which gives the will, and nerves the arm, and brings success, awards a recompense. Among earth's happiest sons, and heaven's most shining saints, devoted laborers hold foremost place.

This lesson ends not here. Phinehas forever stands a noble type. He reflects faith's grand object--salvation's precious champion--Christ Jesus. Yes. Christ is here. In Phinehas, we see Christ's heart, and zeal, and work, and mightily constraining impulse. In

Phinehas we see Christ crowned, too, with the priesthood's glory.

Let thought here pause and commune with salvation's story. What brought Christ from the highest heavens? What led Him, firm amid reproach--unchecked by hindrances--along earth's wretched paths? What nailed Him, a curse, to the accursed tree? They answer well, who say--His love for souls--His burning eagerness to snatch them from hell's flames. But the reply falls short.

True! tender mercy throbbed in His every pulse. But there were mightier motives urging Him with mightier force. The deepest depth was ZEAL FOR GOD. His strongest impulse was to bring glory to His Father's name. Hear His own words, "Lo! I come. I delight to do your will, O my God."

Come, now, view in this light redemption's work. Behold the law--dazzling in purity--wide as infinity in its demands--incapable of change. If it be set aside, God's honor suffers loss. If its decrees are thoroughly fulfilled, God's honor is maintained. Jesus places Himself, as man, beneath its yoke. It asks for nothing, which He gives not. He lives a life of pure compliance. What it exacts, He yields. Can God be honored more? The covenant of grace permits Him to impute this obedience to the ransomed seed--and thus heaven's courts are filled with crowds, in whom no flaw, no speck, no blemish, can be found. All pass those thresholds robed in sinless obedience. Thus Christ exalts God's law. He put on a panoply of zeal, and wrought this magnifying work.

This zeal, too, led Him to the accursed tree. All, whom He saves, are by nature and by act deeply plunged in guilt. Each sin is linked to the unalterable curse. If it descend not, where is God's truth? But Jesus meets it in man's form. Each vial of pledged wrath is outpoured on Him. No sin of His vast family escapes the scourge. Tremendous threats are ratified tremendously. Christ's zeal for God takes the full cup, and drinks it to the dregs. What follows? Justice is just--truth remains true--holiness appears most holy and righteousness most righteous--while grace exults, and mercy sings, and souls are saved, and every attribute is honored.

See then, that God's glory is the brightest jewel in redemption's diadem. The Gospel is Jehovah glorified. If all sin's race had passed to endless woe, justice and truth would have sat sternly on an iron throne--compelling dues--but never satisfied--while loving-kindness would have pined powerless to help. But Jesus's zeal crowns all with glory. Reader, study the Gospel. It is a god-like scheme.

But Phinehas received reward for zeal--even the covenant of everlasting priesthood. So Jesus passed through a low valley to a glorious height. "And being found in appearance as a man, *he humbled himself* and became obedient to death--even death on a cross! Therefore *God exalted him* to the highest place and gave him the name that is above every name." Philip. 2:8-9. "I have glorified You on the earth," is the strong plea. "And now, O Father, glorify me, with Your own self, with the glory which I had with You, before the world was," is the vast prayer. John 17:5.

The plea was mighty, and the prayer was heard. Jesus has turned away eternal wrath. He has brought in eternal reconciliation. Therefore He sits a Priest upon His throne. "All power is given unto Him in heaven and in earth." He sways the scepter of all rule. Thus He consummates redemption's scheme. He takes away the heart of unbelief. He implants love. He engrafts faith. He sows the seeds of righteousness. He waters the tender plants of grace. He matures the precious fruit. He intercedes a conquering Advocate. He perfumes with sweet incense the cry and work of faith. So He, who once laid down His life in zeal, now reigns an all-prevailing Priest.

Believer, such is your Lord. Such was His zeal. Such is His glory. Be then conformed to Him. Let the same mind be the one flame in you. Work for Him--with Him. "It is a faithful saying, For if we have died with Him, we shall also live with Him. If we suffer with Him, we shall also reign with Him."

REFUGE

"Among the cities which you shall give unto the Levites, there shall be six cities for Refuge." Numb. 35:6.

REFUGE is a thought dear to every Christian heart. It is, as haven to the ship, when clouds blacken--as dove-cote to the bird, when hawks pursue. When once the wrath of God is seen in its true light--when once the conscience has turned pale in terror--when once hell's gulf has opened at the feet--when once the quenchless flames have glared in prospect, despair must seize its prey, unless some Refuge be discerned. But Christ a sure Refuge stands, high as the heavens, wide as infinity, lasting as the endless day.

An emblem now is given--seal of this Gospel-fact. Some types of Christ appeared for a brief season, and then vanished. The guiding cloud, the manna, and the flowing stream ended on Jordan's banks. But here is a sign, which lived through Canaan's history. It never failed, until the cross was reared.

The story of the ordinance is brief. The case was possible, that man, without intent--without one evil or revengeful thought, might stain his hands in human blood. An unaimed blow might fall. An undirected arrow might wound fatally. There might be murder unawares.

When such event took place, a kinsman was permitted to arise in wrath, and claim the slayer's life. The law gave license to take blood for blood. He, who had slain, was open to be slain.

Reader, conceive the hapless injurer's state. Peace--happiness--security, were fled forever. Each sight would startle. Each rustling sound would bring alarm. The crowd was peril, for there the kinsman might unsheath his sword. In deep retirement, some ambush might be laid. Thus every spot and every hour would threaten death to the poor trembler's mind. His life was one continual terror.

But Israel's God ordains a means to rescue from such lifelong woe. He bids, that several cities should be set apart. In number they are six. They are distributed throughout the land. Thus no place is very distant from these walls. They stand on lofty hills, conspicuous from afar. They are to be sanctuaries. The manslayer, reaching their Refuge, was at once secure. The angry kinsman

might not enter. The townsmen might not close their gates, by day
nor night--nor cast the fleeing stranger out. Here then security
enclosed him in its arms. Here he might turn and boldly face his
enemy. He had the felt reality of full escape. He knew, that every
danger was left far behind, and that his days might now glide
sweetly, without one shadow of alarm. But he must closely keep
within the covering walls. Outside there still was danger. If he but
stepped beyond the bounds, his life was open to the kinsman's
blow.

He must abide thus sheltered, while the *high-priest* lived. That
death dissolved avenging claims--and then the slayer was at large.
Instantly he might go forth--and unmolested move from place to
place.

It is recorded, that all care was taken to help the slayer in his
flight. Wide roads were formed, and kept in strict repair. All hindrances were smoothed. And at each turn, where doubt might
rise, posts were erected, which on their pointing arms proclaimed,
"Refuge, Refuge!"

Such is the type. Spirit of love, arise to teach! Send forth Your
Christ-revealing light! Grant, that some soul may hence discern
the truth of Gospel-Refuge.

Poor sinner, this type at once displays your case. The slayer is
your counterpart. Perhaps, startled, you cry, "What, are my hands
blood-stained?" In answer take this truth. There may be murder,
though no man be slain. There may be carnage of duties--talents-
-time--souls. And alas! there is. No day, no hour, passes in which
this guilt is not incurred. Earth seems a battle-field, in which we
level blows at God's just claims. It is a charnel-house piled with
the skeletons of slaughtered means of grace. Our words and looks
are often arrows barbed with deathful poison. Who treads not
upon slain opportunities of good? There may not always be pre-
meditation in the sin. *But as the manslayer did not plot his deed,
so sinners blindly commit these murders through ignorance and un-
watched thought.*

Take now the sinner awakened to the sense of this guilt. He is as
the slayer rushing in terror from the kinsman's wrath. He knows
himself to be pursued. Vengeance is pressing at his very heels. An
arm is raised to fell him to the ground. The furious sword is glittering near. The bow is bent. The arrow is poised upon the string.
Another moment, and the fatal wound is given. His mind is agony.
Each fiber quivers. Tremblings beset him. You conscience-strick-
en, say, is not this *your* terrified condition?

One kinsman only hunted the slayer. But many adversaries threaten the guilt-stained soul. Mark the long troop. See, how it rushes on. God's JUSTICE takes the lead. It has strong claims. Its wrongs are many. It has clear right to execute revenge. And it is swift, as God is swift--and strong, as God is strong--and dreadful, as God is dreadful. Can man escape? Ah! sinner, tremble! This foe is near. Its wrath is righteous. Its aim is sure. If you are caught in *nature's plain*, you surely die. If you are clad in nature's armor, you have no safeguard. You must perish.

The LAW is in pursuit, winged with all vengeance. It demands pure unblemished love to God, from the cradle to the grave--from first to last breath--in every child of man, whatever be his station--talent--rank. Exception cannot be. All, who transgress, become its prey. And who transgresses not? Where is the thought, in which love reigns supreme? Where is the moment free from blame? This law must have its dues. It follows sternly. It can never spare. Its curse rolls onward, as a swelling flood, to sweep offenders into the dread abyss. Ah! sinner, tremble! Unless your head has some almighty shelter, you cannot escape.

The TRUTH of God, too, points an inexorable sword. It has decreed, that every sinner must die. Can it recall the righteous word? Can it be false? But false it is, unless the vengeance falls. Sinner, what shield will hide you from this blow?

SATAN moreover follows with huge strides. He claims the sinning soul as his. He has commission to destroy all, who are sin-marked. His eye is keen. His steps have lightning speed. His hate is bitter. He delights to slaughter souls, and drag them to the beds of flames! Ah! sinner, tremble! This cruel foe will surely seize you, unless you reach some shelter higher far than earth--some fortress stronger far than human arm can raise.

These adversaries rush on speedily. Who undismayed can hear their nearing steps? *Thus the fleeing manslayer is a faint shadow of the pursued sinner.* Do any cry, 'where shall we flee? Is there a Refuge?' The question opens the main tidings of this type. Yes. The sheltering cities represent our Refuge. Would that all multitudes, who throng this earth, could hear the blessed truth! Would that a voice of thunder could pervade all lands, proclaiming--'Refuge!' Would that from shore to shore--from hill to hill--from plain to plain, the echo might resound, 'a Refuge is prepared, full--complete--secure!'

Draw near, you guilty sons of men. You need not die. Approach, all you, whom sin oppresses--conscience terrifies--and torturing memory scares. You may be safe. Flee, all who tremble, lest your souls should perish. You may have peace. Fears may be lulled. Anguish may proceed to joy. You may face every foe, and laugh to scorn their every threat. There is a Refuge. It is Christ the Lord. Flee to Him! Flee!

God has been pleased, in wondrous love, in overflowing grace, to set Him as a sheltering sanctuary. The word is pledged, that all in Him are everlastingly secure. "There is therefore now no condemnation to those who are in Christ Jesus." Rom. 8:1.

Let faith now calmly gaze on this city, and mark its TOWERS. Christ's *person* is the grand pillar of security. His strength is full omnipotence. He is Jehovah-Jesus. Who then can snatch from His protecting arms? No one, who is not mightier than God, can burst these gates. While Jesus lives, and lives the mighty God, this safety is complete.

His finished work builds up the Refuge. The walls--the bulwarks of this city--are red with blood. There is inscribed above each gate--"Christ died." Justice draws near. It sees the mark--and asks no more. The wounds of Christ are the deep grave of God's avenging sword. Believer, you may meet justice with the bold challenge, 'Nothing is due from me. My heavenly Surety paid His life for mine. In Him--by Him--I clear your uttermost demand.'

The law's stern curse falls harmless here. It falls, indeed, because it may not be infringed. But Christ receives its weight. And all, locked up in Him, are as unharmed, as Noah within the ark.

Satan pursues up to these gates. But here he pauses. Wherever he finds sin, there he demands his prey. Polluted souls bear mark, that they are his. But all within these walls are washed, and cleansed, and purified, and clothed, and beautified. He must confess, that they are no more his. He must retreat. Their sins are blotted out. Therefore he cannot touch them.

Blessed be God, for this sure Refuge! Reader, imagine every foe in eager chase. See them advancing, in strong flood. Mark their wild rage and frantic hate. Hear their affrighting menaces. See their terrific weapons. Survey the fearsome army. Then rush to Jesus. From all He rescues. From all He shelters. The vilest sinner, nestling in His arms, is safe--safe, as the inhabitants of the highest heaven--safe, as Jehovah on His throne!

Mark, too, this Refuge is AT HAND. In Israel the slayer had to flee oftimes along a tedious road. But our city stands right beside us. At each moment the cry is in our ears, 'Behold Me. Behold Me.' "But the way of getting right with God through faith says, "You don't need to go to heaven" (to find Christ and bring him down to help you). And it says, "You don't need to go to the place of the dead" (to bring Christ back to life again). Salvation that comes from trusting Christ—which is the message we preach—is already within *easy reach.* In fact, the Scriptures say, "The message is *close at hand*; it is on your lips and in your heart." Romans 10:6-8. Outstretched arms invite you. Fall this day within them. The gates are close. Enter this hour. Now all is ready. Oh! linger not. Now is the accepted time.

Believer, you are within this Refuge. You know it to be home of joy unspeakable, and full of glory. Your experience testifies, that its climate is "the peace of God, which passes all understanding." Surely, then, you will cleave tightly to it. Set not one foot beyond the holy precincts. Many temptations will allure you to come forth. Oh! stir not. Abide in Christ. If in unguarded moment you should stray, how instantly some fearful blow is aimed! How suddenly some wound is felt!

Would you be safe through life--in death--forever? Then cleave to Christ, as ivy to the tree, as limpet to the rock. When Israel's high-priest died, the slayer left his shelter. But your High-Priest forever lives, therefore forever you must tarry in your Shelter.

And when you realize your mercies and your safe retreat, can your heart fail to love--your lips to praise--your life to serve? Can you now see such multitudes exposed to wrath, and almost death-struck, and not allure them to your beloved Refuge? Strive, strive, by every means to call them in. Above all, agonize in prayer, that God's all-conquering Spirit may fly speedily throughout earth's bounds, opening blind eyes to see their danger, exciting anxious hearts to rush to this only Refuge.

Printed in the USA
CPSIA information can be obtained
at www.ICGtesting.com
LVHW052205281123
765229LV00050B/1948